DID JESUS USE THE SEPTUAGINT?

David W. Daniels
Artwork by Deborah Daniels

CHICK PUBLICATIONS
Ontario, Calif 91761

Based upon material researched and presented on our YouTube channel, youtube.com/c/chicktracts, from the Was There a B.C. Septuagint? Video series.

For a complete list of distributors near you, call (909) 987-0771, or visit **www.chick.com**

Copyright © 2017 David W. Daniels

Published by:
CHICK PUBLICATIONS
PO Box 3500, Ontario, Calif. 91761-1019 USA
Tel: (909) 987-0771
Fax: (909) 941-8128
Web: www.chick.com
Email: postmaster@chick.com

First Printing

Printed in the United States of America

All rights reserved. No part of this book may be reproduced, stored in a retrieval system or transmitted in any form or by any means (electronic, mechanical, photocopying, recording or otherwise) without permission in writing from the copyright owner.

ISBN: 978-0-75891-1698

Cover Art: This a page of the Codex Vaticanus, Vat.gr.1209_0945_pa_0941
It shows Tobit 11:15 -12:15 in Vaticanus, where it says that alms deliver from death and purge every sin (Tobit 12:09).

Contents

1 Path To A One-World Bible 5

2 'But I Trust the Scholars' 8

3 How Did That Get There? 12

4 Origen-al Sin 30

5 Was There a BC Septuagint? 44

6 Examining the Witnesses of a BC Septuagint 48

7 The 'Christian' Witnesses. 64

8 The Letter of Aristeas. 93

9 The Dead Sea Scrolls. 99

10 The Most Likely Suspect 105

Index 108

THE ARGUMENT

The Argument is simple:

*If Jesus used the Septuagint,
The strategy to create
One World Bible
comes together.
If Jesus didn't use the Septuagint,
Their strategy falls apart.*

*If Jesus used the Septuagint,
Then the Septuagint must be scripture.
Since the Septuagint has the Apocrypha,
The Apocrypha must be scripture.*

*If Jesus did **NOT** use the Septuagint,
The Septuagint is not scripture.
If He used the Hebrew scriptures instead,
He could not use the Apocrypha.*

So the Apocrypha is not scripture.

*To make One World Bible,
They need the Apocrypha.*

*If Jesus didn't use the Septuagint,
There is no basis for adding it to the scriptures to make One World Bible.*

1

Path To A One-World Bible

Increasingly, Christians are buying new Bibles and discovering a surprise tucked inside... publishers are including the Apocrypha in them!

But wait!

- When a family member dies, will you pay to get him out of Purgatory?
- Will you pay alms to get rid of your sins and deliver you from hell?
- Will you pray to angels, when needing guidance or help?

Your new Bible may tell you to.

You will discover that these new additions give you a Bible with so many contradictions, you don't know what to believe! Will you go ask your pastor or priest to make sense of it all?

This is no joke. The Devil wants to take away simple faith in God's holy words. He wants to replace your Bible with his own —a Christ-lowering, faith-destroying, contradictory book that will make you so confused, that you will turn to the church to tell you what to believe.

And then they'll have you. You will be forced to trust Mother Church to interpret everything for you.

The One-World Church is coming for you.

The people who are determined to create a global religion realize that before they can do it, they have to have a one-world Bible compatible with the one-world religion.

They also must get the largest organized religious organization in the world to join it, or they'll never have a world religion. And so they've got to make sure that their Bible for one-world religion includes doctrines that are very important to that organization —the Roman Catholic "church." That means that salvation by works, purgatory, prayer to saints and angels, and other things like that, must be supported by their Bible.

The problem, of course, is that the Bibles that most real Christians use don't have the Apocrypha. So, the Apocrypha has to be worked into it. The way that they've chosen to do that is to come up with a Greek translation of the Old Testament that has the Apocrypha stuck into it and claim that Jesus used it. It's called the Septuagint.

The purpose of this book is to show you where the Septuagint came from and that there is no evidence at all that Jesus and the disciples read the Septuagint. It's fakery. Therefore the Apocrypha is not scripture.

The Old Testament in the Christian Bible is based on the ancient Hebrew scriptures. But the Jews rejected the Apocrypha. They said, "They're not scripture. That's not part of the testament God gave us."

For centuries Christians have also rejected the Apocrypha. They've always said, "The Old Testament is the Jewish scriptures. And therefore they will contain only that which the Jews accept as the scripture." That's why they rejected the

Apocrypha.

But to have a world religion, you've got to have a world Bible. And to have a world Bible, you've got to have the Apocrypha.

To do this, they needed a fake letter to justify their corrupt Bible. They used this approach another time: the Donations of Constantine. It was used to convince rulers that large tracts of land belonged to the Roman Catholic church because they were donated by former rulers. Of course, the former rulers were dead and could not dispute the forged Catholic documents. It was a highly effective strategy.

Modern biblical scholars have turned interest back to this fake Greek document called a Septuagint. They said, "Jesus and the disciples read it. Therefore, they are scripture and you ought to read it, too."

Is that true? Let's find out.

2

'But I Trust the Scholars'

Many Bible believers have been told that without the Roman Catholic Church, we would not have the Bible today. In my book, ***Did the Catholic Church Give Us The Bible?***[1] I show *that there is really two streams of manuscripts in Bible history.* One is, indeed, the source of most modern Bibles.

The other stream is the source of the Classic English version known as the King James Bible. I also show that there are significant differences between them.

Since the KJV has been disparaged for its classic language, and mostly sidelined from the market, the Bibles from the other stream have become the modern Bibles of choice.

*When pastors or leaders are asked why they choose the modern version, they claim that they **trust the scholars** who are recommending the new versions.*

But scholars are fallible men. Dare we trust our eternal life in their hands without a little checking for ourselves? "Scholars" have decided that we arrived here by evolution. That doesn't create a lot of faith in them.

One way to do this is to look at the reliability of the

---

1) *Did the Catholic Church Give Us the Bible? The true history of God's words,* Revised and Expanded Edition (2013), available from Chick Publications.

manuscripts used to produce the Bibles. The stream of manuscripts behind the Classic English KJV is flooded with over 5,700 different copies,[2] all in close agreement as to content. Their histories overlap in a very traceable line back to the early apostles.

The modern versions are based on just a few manuscripts presented as "oldest and best." Oddly, their traceable history only dates back to their "discovery" in the middle of the 19th century. The two primary documents, the Codex Vaticanus and the Codex Sinaiticus, are in the Greek language and are used to produce the modern New Testament portions of the new Bibles.

But they also contain copies of a Greek Old Testament document that has been identified as the "Septuagint." Scholars claim that it originated three centuries before Christ and was actually read by Jesus and the apostles in the early church.

The odd thing about the Septuagint is that it contains books, called the "Apocrypha," that are not in the Hebrew Old Testament. These are fictional or legendary stories more or less set in a historical context. These stories have been woven into Roman Catholic Bibles ever since the 5th century, when they were translated into Latin. And a number of unbiblical Roman doctrines are based on them.

It's been going on quietly, but all around us leaders have been trying to get us to trust the Septuagint, a Greek Old Testament. Some tell you, "Jesus and the apostles read it and quoted it, so you should, too!"

---

2) That's over 5,700 copies of Greek texts for the New Testament alone. It doesn't count other early translations or any of the Old Testament manuscripts.

Did you know that every missionary Bible translation under the United Bible Societies, Wycliffe Bible Translators, SIL and many others, was made with the requirement that the translators must add the Apocrypha if the people request it?

And, as I described in my book, ***Why They Changed the Bible,*** on many mission fields, Roman Catholics and evangelical Protestants are working side by side in the translation world. In fact, in 1966 a common Greek text was agreed upon to be used as the foundation of all translations. And where Roman Catholics request it, the Apocrypha must be included in the newly translated Bible for that language group.[3]

But the Apocrypha didn't come from the Hebrew Bible. It came from the Septuagint, from Alexandria, Egypt. And did you know that it contains writings in favor of: praying for the dead, purgatory, committing suicide, an angel of God lying, sorcery and magic?

How could Jesus quote something that contradicts other scripture?

The Septuagint was also used as the basis for the Roman Catholic Bible, the Roman Catholic Latin Vulgate, used by the Catholic Church from 405 AD to 1970, and in English in the Douay-Rheims, as well.

The other abundant stream of manuscripts, that backs the Classic English KJV, does not depend on this contaminated Septuagint Old Testament. Instead, it comes from the Hebrew Masoretic Text, so carefully preserved by centuries of Hebrew scribes.

---

3) See *Why They Changed the Bible: One World Bible for One World Religion* (2014), pp. 105-107, 115-117, 120-121, 237-238, 250, 252-253. Available from Chick Publications.

Should we abandon this and read the Septuagint instead? Or is there something wrong with this whole push?

What is the proof that the Septuagint was written ***before Christ***, anyway? It turns out that the evidence goes back to just one letter, called the *Letter of Aristeas*. Is that letter real, or fake? And is there any other evidence to help us decide?

Examine the ***best evidence*** yourself for a BC Septuagint, one that supposedly ***existed before Christ,*** in the following chapters.

Let's see where the evidence takes us.

3

How Did That Get There?

Where did the Vaticanus and Sinaiticus come from?

When we trace back through the Alexandrian (southern) stream of Bible manuscripts, we find the legend of a Greek Old Testament called the "Septuagint." Scholars like to say it was made about 285 BC. But, like most of the other documents in this polluted stream, once you ask some basic questions, you start to doubt the official story of its age —and of its being "oldest and best."

As you will see, Roman Catholic leaders have claimed for ages that this Septuagint was the Greek Bible (Old Testament) that Jesus and the apostles used and quoted.

New technology available today is bringing to light long-hidden information about the key documents of Bible history and the individuals who were involved.

Tischendorf, for example, became the central figure of the two documents considered "oldest and best," Codex (big book) Sinaiticus and Codex Vaticanus in the mid-1800s.

Long before that, Origen was a prominent figure in the early to mid-200s, who appears to have been involved with the Septuagint as we find it today.

Figure 1. Origen of Alexandria (184-254 AD).

What kind of man was Origen? He lived from about 184 to 254 AD. He is largely responsible for the beginning of the polluted stream of Bibles that spread from Alexandria, Egypt.

Look at what he said about God and the Bible in his most famous book, *"De Principiis," On First Principles,* quoted in *The Church Fathers on the Bible,* by Catholic Frank Sadowski.[4] They're long quotes, so I'll summarize them here.

First, Origen said that "the Word of God" (Jesus) stuck "certain stumbling blocks" and "impossibilities" into the Bible. There was some real history, but Jesus added "mystical senses" to the historical events. And then Jesus hid that "deeper meaning" from the multitude. So Origen thought the common folk were ignorant and unworthy of these secret, mystical meanings.

But he said the Scripture also added stories of events "that

---

4) See *The Church Fathers on the Bible: Selected Readings,* Edited by Frank Sadowski, S.S.P (New York: Alba House, Society of St. Paul, 1987), Chapter 24, Origen, "On 1st Principles" 4:8-19, pp. 121-125. All emphasis mine.

did not take place, sometimes what ***could not*** have happened; sometimes what ***could, but did not***." Origen said that Jesus put ***lies*** in the Bible, on purpose. He called Jesus a ***liar!***

Then he blamed the Spirit! Origen said that the Spirit wove into the Gospels and the Epistles events that are written as if they happened, "but which ***did not actually occur***." Then he said that even "the law and the commandments" are not reasonable.

He said that "…those who are not altogether blind can collect countless instances" of events "recorded as having occurred, but which ***did not literally take place***"!

*He doesn't sound like a Bible-believer, does he? He sounds more like a Bible-**doubter**. And yet some say he was the early church's greatest theologian and text scholar.*

It is said that Origen spent up to 20 years to make one gigantic book. It took maybe 40-50 codices the size of the Sinaiticus to hold it all, and it's said that he used slaves to help him make it. He took at least 6 complete Greek Old Testaments (at least 2 with the Apocrypha) that existed at that time, and arranged them in 6 columns, side by side. This is what was called "the Hexapla" (six-ply).

It appears that one of the columns was the "Septuagint," (that contains the Apocrypha) which modern scholars claim to be the Bible (Old Testament) that Jesus and the Apostles used. It is also the Greek document that Rome translated into Latin to make the Old Testament portion of the Roman Catholic Latin Vulgate which became the basis of the English Douay-Rheims Bible, used in Western Catholic Churches until the middle of the 20th century. Of course, all of the Catholic Bibles included the Apocrypha.

Origen's personal decisions directly affected the content of the Septuagint (and thus the later Bibles based on it). And whoever created the other two key manuscripts, the Sinaiticus and Vaticanus, that all modern versions depend on, were affected by those decisions, as well.

Modern technology has made a way to research these documents like never before. And guess what? There's a lot of fakery involved. Let me show you how it's done.

Let's use a perfect example of a fraud: the Book of Mormon. One way I can tell the Book of Mormon is a fake, is simply to read the King James Bible. Just this morning I opened a Book of Mormon to a random page. This is in 2 Nephi. The note at the bottom says this was written "between 559 and 545 B.C." But listen to these phrases:

From 9:6, "For as death hath passed upon all men" … "and the fall came by reason of transgression"

From 9:7, "this corruption could not put on incorruption"

From 9:9, about the Devil, "who transformeth himself nigh unto an angel of light"

So in 3 verses, this supposedly 550s BC Book of Mormon has taken words right out of Romans 5:12, 5:14, 1 Corinthians 15:53 and 2 Corinthians 11:14-15. That's quite a feat to write the Apostle Paul's words, 600 years before Paul did!

*But what if I could show you where the Greek Old Testament, that they call the "Septuagint," supposedly written in **285 BC**, copied 48 words in a row from the Apostle Paul's letter to the Romans (57-58 AD), into the Psalms, which David originally wrote 1,000 years earlier?*

I know that was a complex sentence. But please realize this. Trying to explain the creation of the Septuagint Greek

Old Testament is like trying to eat an elephant. So let me take this just one tiny bite at a time.

*Why is this important? Because remember, this supposedly "285 BC" Greek Old Testament, called the Septuagint, has been said by Roman Catholics and other professors to have **more authority than the Hebrew**, because they say it was the Bible used by Jesus and the apostles!*

Because of that, Roman Catholics said it was inspired. Then they took that "Septuagint" Greek Old Testament and had it translated into Latin. That Latin became the Old Testament of the Roman Catholic Latin Vulgate. And that Roman Catholic Latin Vulgate was later translated by Jesuits into an English Bible in 1582-1610 and called the Douay-Rheims Bible.

Some of you may have family members who still have a Douay-Rheims. It comes directly from the Roman Catholic Latin Vulgate, which comes directly from the Greek Septuagint Old Testament, plus the Alexandrian Greek New Testament.

> **Greek Septuagint (+Alexandrian NT)**
> becomes
> **Catholic Latin Vulgate**
> becomes
> **English Douay-Rheims**

*The Catholic Bible **didn't** go back to the Hebrew. It only went back to the "Septuagint" **Greek** Old Testament.*

That's why it is so important to know which Jesus used: the Septuagint or the Hebrew scriptures.

Here's a Catholic claim for the Septuagint. In the Preface

of the 1914 edition of the Douay-Rheims it says: "...the *Septuagint*, the Greek translation from the original Hebrew, and which contained all the writings now found in the Douay version, as it is called, ***was* the *version*** used by the Saviour and his Apostles and by the Church from her infancy, and translated into Latin, known under the title of Latin Vulgate, and ***ever recognized as the true version of the written word of God***."[5]

*That's how they all fit together. And notice, these versions **always included** those legends and folk tales of the Apocrypha.*

If I can show you where Paul's words were clearly quoted from the New Testament, written sometime around the 50s AD, and inserted into the Psalms of David, from 1000 years earlier, then this Septuagint is just as fake as the Book of Mormon.

So now, open your Bible to Romans 3:10-12: "As it is written, There is none righteous, no, not one: There is none that understandeth, there is none that seeketh after God. They are all gone out of the way, they are together become unprofitable; there is none that doeth good, no, not one."

Now Paul is summarizing Psalm 14:1-3. It's not a *quote* —it's a *summary*. Check it for yourself, later.

Then from verses 13-18, Paul **summarized** other verses that also say none is righteous, specifically Psalms 5:10; 139:4; 9:28; Isaiah 59:7-8; and Psalm 35:2. Look at his words in these 6 verses:

"Their throat *is* an open sepulchre; with their tongues

---

5) *The Holy Bible, Translated from the Latin Vulgate, etc.*, published with the Approbation of James Cardinal Gibbons, Archbishop of Baltimore (1899, reprint 1914), Preface, p. i. Emphasis mine.

they have used deceit; the poison of asps *is* under their lips: Whose mouth *is* full of cursing and bitterness: Their feet *are* swift to shed blood: Destruction and misery *are* in their ways: And the way of peace have they not known: There is no fear of God before their eyes."

Now, not one of Paul's 6 verses from Romans is in the Hebrew of Psalm 14. The Holy Ghost wrote those words through the apostle Paul, not King David.

I made a chart of these verses, and compared the Received Text Greek and the King James English to the codices Vaticanus, Sinaiticus and Alexandrinus —the same Greek Bibles that are used to **create** the modern so-called "Septuagint." You see, the original Septuagint does not exist. The copies called the Septuagint today are simply created out of a blend of the Vaticanus, Sinaiticus and Alexandrinus.

How Did That Get There?

Romans 3:13-18 King James	Romans 3:13-18 Received Text	Romans 3:13-18 Vaticanus (M-03A)	Romans 3:13-18 Sinaiticus (M-01A)	Romans 3:13-18 Alexandrinus (M-02A)
13 Their throat is an open sepulchre; with their tongues they have used deceit; the poison of asps is under their lips:	τάφος ἀνεῳγμένος ὁ λάρυγξ αὐτῶν ταῖς γλώσσαις αὐτῶν ἐδολιοῦσαν ἰὸς ἀσπίδων ὑπὸ τὰ χείλη αὐτῶν· (STE)	ταφος ανεωγμενος ο λαρυγξ αυτων ταις γλωσσαις αυτων εδολιουσαν ιος ασπιδω¯ υπο τα χειλη αυτων	ταφος ανεωγμενος ο λαρυγξ αυτω¯ ταις γλωσσαις αυτων εδολιουσαν ιος ασπιδων υπο τα χυλη αυτων	ταφος ανεωγμενος ο λαρυγξ αυτω¯ ταις γλωσσαις αυτων εδολιουσα¯ ιος ασπιδων υπο τα χειλη αυτω¯
14 Whose mouth is full of cursing and bitterness:	ὧν τὸ στόμα ἀρᾶς καὶ πικρίας γέμει	ων το στομα αυτων αρας και πικριας γεμει	ων το στομα αρας και πικριας γεμει	ων το στομα αρας και πικριας γεμει
15 Their feet are swift to shed blood:	ὀξεῖς οἱ πόδες αὐτῶν ἐκχέαι αἷμα	οξεις οι ποδες αυτω¯ εκχεαι αιμα	οξεις οι ποδες αυτων εκχεαι αιμα	οξεις οι ποδες αυτων εκχεαι αιμα
16 Destruction and misery are in their ways:	σύντριμμα καὶ ταλαιπωρία ἐν ταῖς ὁδοῖς αὐτῶν	συντριμμα και ταλαιπωρια εν ταις οδοις αυτων	συντριμμα και ταλαιπωρια εν ταις οδοις αυτων	συντριμμα και ταλαιπωρια ε¯ ταις οδοις αυτων
17 And the way of peace have they not known:	καὶ ὁδὸν εἰρήνης οὐκ ἔγνωσαν	και οδον ειρηνης ουκ εγνωσαν	και οδον ιρηνης ουκ εγνωσαν	και οδον ειρηνης ουκ εγνωσαν
18 There is no fear of God before their eyes.	οὐκ ἔστιν φόβος θεοῦ ἀπέναντι τῶν ὀφθαλμῶν αὐτῶν	ουκ <u>εστιν</u> φοβος ōῡ απεναντι των οφθαλμων αυτων	ουκ εστι¯ φοβος ōῡ απεναντι των οφθαλμω¯ αυτων	ουκ εστιν φοβος ōῡ απεναντι των οφθαλμων αυτων
		εστι: εστι		
	48 Greek words	49 Greek words	48 Greek words	48 Greek words

Figure 2. Comparison table of Romans 3:13-18 in various Greek texts.

Paul's words in Romans 3:13-18 add up to *48* Greek words. The above chart shows how these verses of Romans are ***almost exactly identical*** in the three main Greek codices (big books), Vaticanus, Sinaiticus and Alexandrinus.

Both Sinaiticus and Alexandrinus have Paul's words in

Romans 3:13-18, word for word.

Vaticanus accidentally added one additional word, but all 48 of Paul's words are still there.

*It's one of the **only** places where so many words agree in these Bibles!*

That's because they copied **Paul's exact Greek words** into the Septuagint Old Testament, at Psalm 14:3. They wouldn't alter Paul's words here, because *they wanted them to match!*

So now let's look at Psalm 14:3. (In the Greek Septuagint, it is 13:3.) Here it is in the King James:

"They are all gone aside, they are altogether become filthy; there is none that doeth good, no, not one."

That's the end. There are no more words.

But look at Vaticanus.

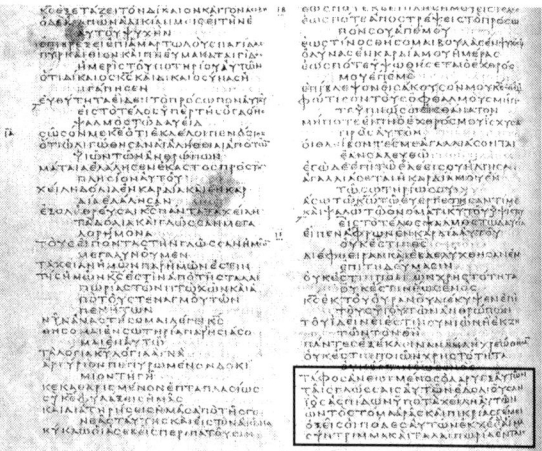

Figure 3. Psalm 13:3 in Vaticanus containing Romans 3:13-18.

How Did That Get There? 21

Figure 4. Balance of Psalm 13:3 in Vaticanus.

You see those words inside the box, on the last column of one page and the first column of the next?

Here's a close-up of those words in the Psalm:

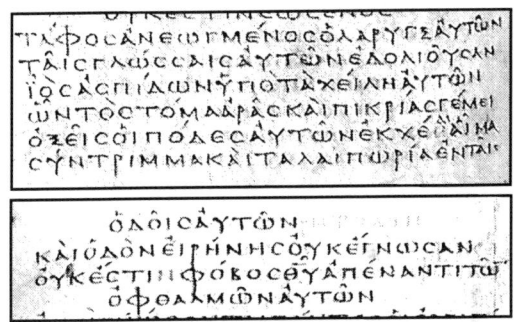

Figure 5. Close-up of Psalm 13:3 from Vaticanus.

Those are uncial (upper case) letters of the ***exact same words*** Paul wrote in Romans 3![6]

And what about the Sinaiticus?

---

6) See Figure 2 above.

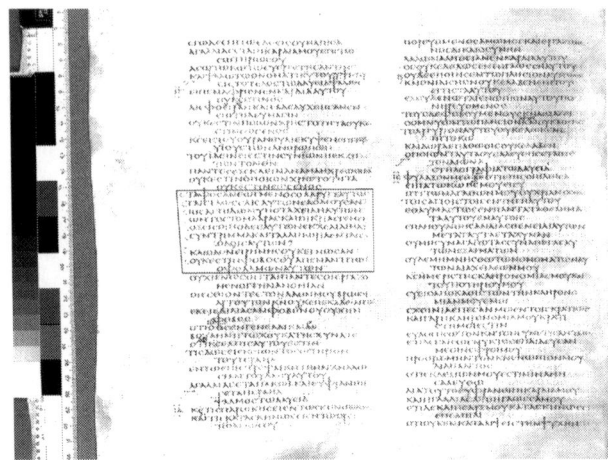

Figure 6. Romans 3:13-18 inserted into Psalm 13:3 in Sinaiticus

There they are in the text, plain as day. Look at it up close. The letters are identical to Vaticanus:

Figure 7. Close-up of Psalm 13:3 from Sinaiticus.

Do you see those brackets left and right, like forward and backward Cs? Somebody added those marks around these words.

Because of those brackets, the codexsinaiticus.org website

How Did That Get There? 23

put all 48 words in purple font, to set them apart:

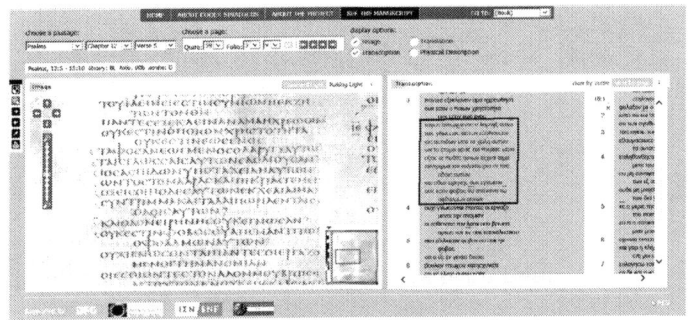

Figure 8. Codexsinaiticus.org web page with 48 words of Psalm 13:3 flagged.

They are saying the brackets mean those words were "deleted." But they weren't deleted by the guy who originally copied down the text. And the guy who wrote the Greek there is Scribe D, the boss corrector.

So ***somebody else*** had to put the correction marks there, after the Psalm was copied into the Sinaiticus. They weren't originally there.

*Regardless, you can see Paul's words from the 50s AD, clearly put into Psalm 14, a psalm David originally wrote in Hebrew 1,000 years earlier. Paul's words are **right there** in the Greek Old Testament of both Sinaiticus and Vaticanus.*

Those ***same words*** were translated into **Latin** for the Catholic Vulgate, and into **English** for the Douay-Rheims.

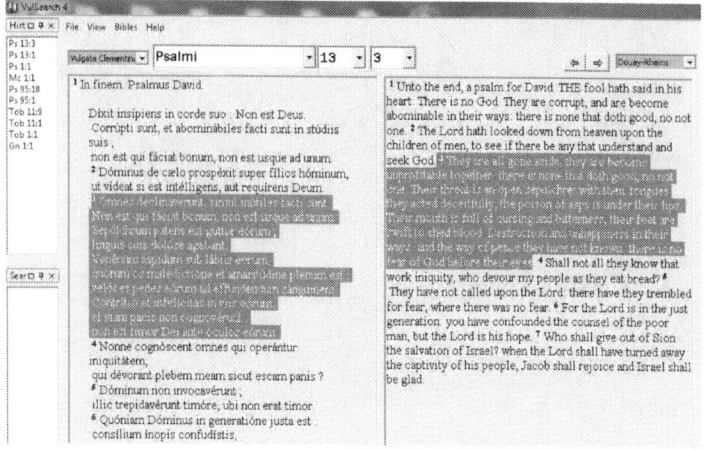

Figure 9. Psalm 14:3 (13:3) additions from Romans 3:13-18, in the Latin Catholic Vulgate (left) and English Catholic Douay-Rheims (right).

Out of the three codices, it turns out that Alexandrinus is the only one that **doesn't** have those extra words. This is proved in the footnotes of the Rahlfs-Hanhart *Septuaginta* of 2006, the authoritative ***modern*** Septuagint text. At this verse, it has a footnote that says ">A." That means these words of Paul's are "omitted in Alexandrinus."

13 (𝔐 14) 1 tit. ψ. / τω δ.] tr. S | 1^2 διεφθαρησαν A || 3^2 ποιων] pr. ο S | 3^{3-10} > A: ex Rom. 3 13–18, ubi Paulus haec uerba (= Ps. 5 10 139 4 9 28 Is. 59 7.8 Ps. 35 2) cum Ps. 13 3 iunxit || 4^1 ανομιαν] αδικιαν B† | 4^2 κατεσθιοντες] ι > B, κατ > S | βρωσει] pr. εν A || 5^1 φοβω] -βον S | ου] ω A 5^2 δικαιων A || 7^3 αγαλλιασεται et ευφρανθησεται SA
14 (𝔐 15) 1^2 και] η A | τω 1^0 > A

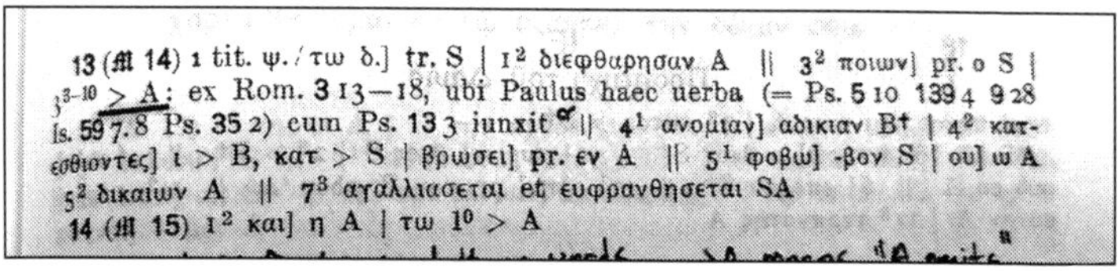

Figure 10. Excerpt from *Septuaginta* of Psalm 14:3 (13:3) with note about Paul's words added from Romans 3:13-18.

The Latin words after that, "ex Rom. 3:13-18, ubi Paulus haec uerba (= Ps. 5:10; 139:4; 9:28; Is. 59:7, 8; Ps. 35:2) cum

Ps. 13:3 iunxit" mean this:

"from Romans 3:13-18, where Paul these words" (then it lists the various scriptures Paul referenced) "joined with Psalm 13:3." So even the *Septuaginta* openly admits that they know the words were joined by Paul, not David.

But it's not just the modern book that says those words are added from Paul. Look at the Hexapla made by Origen in the 230s AD.[7]

> 3. הַכֹּל סָר יַחְדָּו. *Numquid omnis deflexit una?*
> Ο'. πάντες ἐξέκλιναν ἅμα. 'Α. ἕκαστος ἀπέστη ἅμα.[6]
>
> Ο'. ÷ τάφος ἀνεῳγμένος ——— τῶν ὀφθαλμῶν αὐτῶν ⌐.[7]

Figure 11. Origen's Hexapla note on Paul's words in Psalm 13:3.

The O' at the beginning means "Origen's column of the Hexapla." Look at the second O'. Right after that, see the ÷ at the beginning, the long ——— dash in the middle, and the angled ⌐ sign at the end? They were Origen's way of marking off a whole section of words. He was saying these words are not in the Hebrew text. That meant they didn't really belong in the Greek, either.

---

7) See *Origenis Hexaplorum Quae Supersunt... Vetus Testamentum Fragmenta* [*Origen's Hexapla Which Remains: or, fragments of first interpreters of the Greeks on the entire Old Testament*], edited by Frederick Field (Oxford: Clarendon Press, 1875), p. 165.

> ÷marks "The beginning of what was in the Greek, but not in the Hebrew."
>
> ——"This is like putting ellipses (…) between words in a sentence. It is used instead of the words in between."
>
> An angled ⊥marks "The ending of what was in the Greek, but not in the Hebrew."

Look at those Greek words. Those are the beginning and ending of all those added words from Romans! ***So Origen himself knew and admitted*** that those 48 words did ***not*** come from the Psalms, at all. Somebody added them, copying from Paul's letter to the Romans.

You can see those words in the *Septuaginta*. They are in the text, but with brackets.

How Did That Get There?

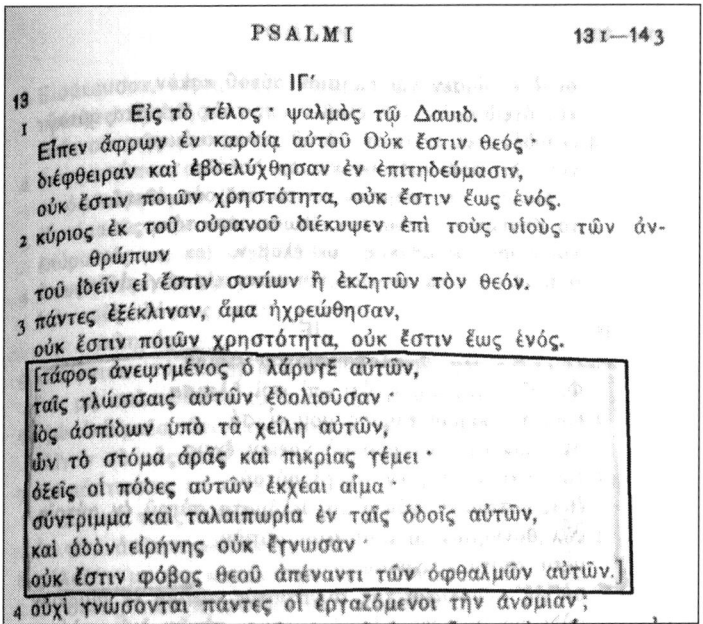

Figure 12. Psalm 14:3 (13:3) in Rahlf's *Septuaginta* (2006).

So that is what you find in some of the Greek Old Testaments that they call the "Septuagint." *48 of Paul's words are moved backwards in time and stuck into a 1,000 year-old Psalm in both Vaticanus and Sinaiticus.* Then those **added words** were translated into Latin in Jerome's Roman Catholic Latin Vulgate, and into English in every copy of the official Douay-Rheims Catholic Bible. The Catholic leaders kept them in the text, until they finally no longer needed them.

That was when they got together with Protestants and Baptists to make one world Hebrew Old Testament and one world Greek New Testament, and a brand-new one-world Latin Catholic Bible, the 1979 *Nova Vulgata*, that matched them both.[8] After that, the Catholic Bibles then started to look more like the modern "Critical Text" Bibles, such as the Catholic New American Bible of 1970 and almost all new Protestant Bibles —except Catholic Bibles which insisted upon the Apocrypha, as well.

The Apostle Paul's words could not possibly have been written before Christ came, in a BC Septuagint or anywhere else. The only way you could find them in a Greek Old Testament is if someone created the Septuagint (or modified it) **after** Paul's letters were spread to the churches.

*I've been saying for years that the so-called "Septuagint," the Greek Old Testament, had to be written **after** the New Testament, because New Testament verses and words are stuck into Old Testament verses. The only way to do that is if you have a New Testament sitting **in front of you**.*

There are other examples I could show you of this. I've already showed you that ancient writers and even modern scholars admit it!

This is what we've learned:

The Book of Mormon was written *after* the New Testament.

The so-called Greek "Septuagint" was also written *after* the New Testament.

Jesus didn't use that Septuagint.

The Apostles didn't use that Septuagint.

We don't have *a single copy* of a Greek Septuagint from before the 300s AD at the earliest. The first bits that we have of a Septuagint Greek Old Testament are from copies

---

8) See *Why They Changed the Bible* (2014), pp. 199-201. Available from Chick Publications.

of parts of Origen's *Hexapla*.

*Any book we have today that is **called** the "Septuagint" is really just a modern book that is made up of a blending together of the Old Testament sections of three big Greek books: Codices Alexandrinus, Vaticanus and Sinaiticus.*

Even in the notes that were taken from Origen's *Hexapla*, all that remains of his 20 years of work, Origen indicated clearly that those 48 words of Paul's ***didn't belong*** in the Old Testament. It would be a lie to say they did belong.

Origin **clearly noted** that Paul's words ***shouldn't*** be there. But Origen wrote a letter that said the Septuagint should stay as it is.[9] How that happened, and what Origen said, as well as what Augustine and Jerome wrote, you will find out later in this book.

It is no easy task to try to figure out the original words that were written in the Septuagint. All we really have are copies of documents from at least the 300s AD, well after Origen got his hands on them.

Thank God I don't have to try to reconstruct which words are God's words and which are not.

I have the words that were spread all over the world by faithful believers. I have the words that God blessed, as they were translated into hundreds of languages. I have the words that bring faith, not doubt.

That's because I have God's perfectly preserved words in Classic, timeless English, the King James Bible.

The origin of ***these words***, is God Himself!

---

9) See Chapter 4, Origen-al Sin.

4

Origen-al Sin

What do you do with a liar? Don't trust him any further than you can ***check him***.

Here's a lie: "We have the Septuagint."

No, we don't.

What they call the "Septuagint" is supposed to be a Greek Old Testament mixed with Apocrypha, that was supposedly created by 72 translators in Alexandria, Egypt, starting in 285 BC. Then the story goes that Jesus and the apostles quoted from that Septuagint Old Testament, and not the Hebrew.

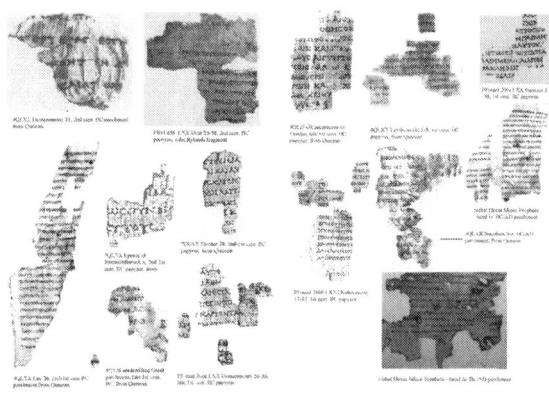

Figure 13. Dead Sea Scraps – bits of Old Testament verses in Greek.

Origen-al Sin 31

*Here's the problem. We don't have **any** copies, anywhere, of more than just a few Greek Old Testament words. You couldn't make a "Septuagint" out of them.*

Figure 14. My copy of *The Septuagint with Apocrypha*.

This is my copy of *The Septuagint with Apocrypha*, that I got at Fuller Seminary. It was originally published in 1851. This couldn't have been the Bible ***they say*** Jesus used, either. Lancelot Brenton claimed he made this book from the Codex Vaticanus, with a little out of the Codex Alexandrinus, where Vaticanus was missing something. Everyone dates those big books as being made ***at least*** 300-500 years ***after*** Jesus.

My professors said "Your Septuagint isn't the best one. You need the Critical Text." Alright then. So I bought one.

It's the critical text, the Rahlfs-Hanhart *Septuaginta* from 2006. It's been slightly updated from the 1935 edition.

Figure 15. Old Testament Greek Critical Text: Rahlfs-Hanhart *Septuaginta*.

Jesus didn't use ***this*** book, either. It's actually a blending of the text critics' 3 favorite codices: Alexandrinus, Vaticanus, and Sinaiticus. Again, those big books were all written no less than three centuries ***after*** Jesus, not before.

Figure 16. Origen, Creator of the Hexapla.

It's also partly based upon readings from something called the *Hexapla*. And that takes us to a liar named Origen. This one guy may actually be the ***origin*** of the messed-up so-called "Septuagint" in the ***form*** we find it today, as we see it in the Alexandrinus, the Vaticanus, and the Sinaiticus. And that origin —is the liar, Origen. Be very careful when you study Origen. Don't believe anything you can't prove.

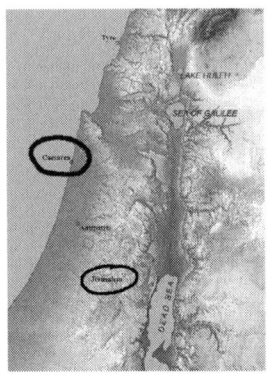

Figure 17. Caesarea Maritima, 70 miles from Jerusalem.

Origen is the father of modern, doubting Bibles. He lived almost 70 years, from about 184 to 254 AD. He spent his young life in Alexandria, Egypt. The last 24 years he lived in Caesarea Maritima, 70 miles northwest of Jerusalem. That's where he put together the *Hexapla*. I'll tell more on that later.

Origen-al Sin 33

Figure 18. Eusebius, Constantine's lapdog.

According to Constantine's lapdog, Eusebius, in 203 AD Origen re-started the Catechetical School of Alexandria, as a young man of 18-19. It was a school of exegesis and theology, similar to a seminary. Origen became extremely popular.

I have said in the past that I suspected the only way Origen could write the many books people said he did, is if he had stenographers to write everything he said, practically 24/7, like the Mormon Joseph Smith and later Brigham Young did in the 1800s. Well, guess what? He did!

A wealthy convert named Ambrose gave Origen at least **7 stenographers** to write every word he said, **7 longhand scribes** to make them into books, as well as **ladies** to make copies of those books. So he could just talk away and they'd write it down and publish it for him. So ***that's*** how he "wrote" over 2,000 books. He didn't really write them. He ***dictated them***.

Origen was popular. But Origen was elitist, as well. Origen believed that there were some secrets (or many) that only higher-level scholars, or initiates into his private religion, should know.

We know this from his own writings and from people who claimed to follow his teachings.

For instance, Madame Blavatsky, who founded the occultic religion Theosophy, said this in her book, *Isis Unveiled*:

Figure 19. Madame Blavatsky and her book, *Isis Unveiled*.

"Origen, who had belonged to the Alexandrian school of Platonists, declares that Moses, besides the teachings of the covenant, communicated some very important *secrets* 'from the hidden depths of the law' to the seventy elders. ***These he enjoined [commanded] them to impart only to persons whom they found worthy.***"[10]

She also wrote that Origen and Clement of Alexandria before him, "…were well versed in Pagan symbology, having begun their careers as philosophers…"[11] I found out that, when Origen saw a student who showed promise, he'd also

---

10) *Isis Unveiled,* Vol. 1, by Helena Petrovna Blavatsky (New York: JW Bouton, 1891), pp. 25-26. Emphasis mine.
11) *Isis Unveiled,* Vol. 1, p. 298.

teach him geometry and philosophy.

Walter Walsh, in ***The Secret History of the Oxford Movement*** (about 1897), revealed that "in the Church of Alexandria, the Catechumens [the students] were *not* taught *all* the doctrines of the Christian Faith. Many of these were treated by their teachers as *secret* doctrines to be held in *reserve*."[12]

This "Doctrine of Reserve" from Clement of Alexandria and Origen after him, taught that it was okay to *lie* to their students, if they weren't "worthy" or ready for the "deeper secrets of God." So people that Origen felt were unworthy could be left in the dark, or ***allowed to believe lies***, because only the scholars or spiritually advanced were permitted to learn the esoteric, secret doctrines.

That is the same "Doctrine of Reserve" that was used in England. Hundreds of secretly-ordained Catholic priests pretended to be Protestants in the 1800s. Walsh quotes from the Roman *Catholic Standard and Ransomer,* edited by a priest who was once a Protestant minister, dated November 22nd, 1894. "We have heard just lately that there are now ***eight hundred*** clergymen of the Church of England who have been ***validly*** ordained by Dr. Lee and his co-Bishops of the Order of Corporate Reunion…."[13]

In other words, they were secretly re-ordained Catholics, while still looking like Protestants. And this lying ***Doctrine of Reserve*** has been a ***big doctrine*** of the Jesuit Order, from its founding in the 1540s to the present day.

But wait. Didn't Origen also give us that text-scholarly *Hexapla,* the 6-columned Old Testament, which had

---

12) *The Secret History of the Oxford Movement*, by Walter Walsh (London: Swan Sonnenschein & Co., Ltd., 5th edition, 1899), p. 2. Emphasis mine.
13) *The Secret History of the Oxford Movement*, p. 161. Emphasis original.

Hebrew, 3 different Greek versions, and the Septuagint?

One of my friends said to me, "He sounds like a person who would *preserve* the text, not change it." You're right. He does **sound** like that. But Origen's ***Doctrine of Reserve*** means that he could admit what he truly believed, or truly researched, to a few elite people, and lie to the rest, because he thought they were "unworthy." Watch how this plays out.

Origen made a big book, the Hexapla, as I said before, containing six complete Old Testaments. It was so huge, thousands of pages, that only one was ever made, and it took him (even with all that help) over 20 years to make it.

Here's what it sort-of looked like:

Hebrew.	Hebrew Transliterated.	Aquila.	Symmachus.	LXX.	Theodotion.	Variants.
לַמְנַצֵּחַ	λαμανασσημ	τῷ νικοποιῷ	ἐπινίκιος	εἰς τὸ τέλος	τῷ νικοποιῷ	εἰς τὸ τέλος
לִבְנֵי קֹרַח	βνη κορα	τῶν υἱῶν κορέ	τῶν υἱῶν κορέ	ὑπὲρ τῶν υἱῶν κορέ (τοῖς υἱοῖς)	τοῖς υἱοῖς κορέ	
עַל־עֲלָמוֹת	αλ· αλαμωθ	ἐπὶ νεανιοτήτων	ὑπὲρ τῶν αἰωνίων	ὑπὲρ τῶν κρυφίων	ὑπὲρ τῶν κρυφίων	
שִׁיר	σιρ	ἄσμα	ᾠδή·	ψαλμός	ᾠδή	ψαλμός
אֱלֹהִים לָנוּ	ελωειμ λανου	<ὁ θεὸς ἡμῖν>	ὁ θεὸς ἡμῖν	ὁ θεὸς ἡμῶν	ὁ θεὸς ἡμῶν	
מַחֲסֶה וָעֹז	μασσε· ουος	ἐλπὶς καὶ κράτος	πεποίθησις καὶ ἰσχύς	καταφυγὴ καὶ δύναμις	καταφυγὴ καὶ δύναμις	
עֶזְרָה	εζρ	βοήθεια	βοήθεια	βοηθὸς	βοηθὸς	
בְצָרוֹת	βσαρωθ	ἐν θλίψεσιν	ἐν θλίψεσιν	ἐν θλίψεσι	ἐν θλίψεσιν	
נִמְצָא מְאֹד	νεμσα· μωδ	εὑρεθεὶς σφόδρα	εὑρισκόμενος σφόδρα	ταῖς εὑρούσαις ἡμᾶς σφόδρα (εὑρεθήσεται ἡμῖν)	εὑρέθη σφόδρα (ταῖς εὑρούσαις ἡμᾶς)	
עַל־כֵּן	αλ· χεν	ἐπὶ τούτῳ	διὰ τοῦτο	διὰ τοῦτο	διὰ τοῦτο	
לֹא נִירָא	λω· νιρα	οὐ φοβηθησόμεθα	οὐ φοβηθησόμεθα	οὐ φοβηθησόμεθα	οὐ φοβηθησόμεθα	
בְּהָמִיר	βεαμιρ	ἐν τῷ ἀνταλλάσσεσθαι	ἐν τῷ συγχεῖσθαι	ἐν τῷ ταράσσεσθαι	ἐν τῷ ταράσσεσθαι	
אֶרֶץ	[a]αρσ	γῆν	γῆν	τὴν γῆν	τὴν γῆν	
וּבְמוֹט	ου βαμοτ	καὶ ἐν τῷ σφάλλεσθαι	καὶ κλίνασθαι	καὶ μετατίθεσθαι	καὶ σαλεύεσθαι (μετατίθεσθαι)	
הָרִים	αριμ	ὄρη	ὄρη	ὄρη	ὄρη	
בְּלֵב	βλεβ	ἐν καρδίᾳ	ἐν καρδίᾳ	ἐν καρδίᾳ	ἐν καρδίᾳ	
יַמִּים:	ιαμιμ	θαλασσῶν	θαλασσῶν	θαλασσῶν	θαλασσῶν	

Figure 20. What Origen's *Hexapla* may have looked like.

To fit all 6 columns, only one or two words could be on each line. Column 1 was Hebrew, written with Hebrew letters. Column 2 was the same Hebrew, written with Greek letters. Column 3 was a translation of the Hebrew into Greek by Aquila, a convert to Judaism. Jewish scholars say it was literal —but so literal it didn't always make sense in Greek. That was done about 120-130 AD.

Column 4 was a totally different Greek translation of the Hebrew by Symmachus. He did it about 170-200 AD. Column 6 was a very "free" translation by Theodotion. Jewish scholars say he didn't really know Hebrew, and probably went from Greek to Greek. He wrote about the same time as Symmachus.

And that brings us to Column 5 that was done by Origen, and all the texts I can find say it was marked with an O′ — for Origen. It was not marked with "LXX," the symbol for the Septuagint.[14]

Origen spent a couple decades working on this huge set of books.

He marked what was the commonly used Greek text in Alexandria with two signs, called the asterisk, or *metobelus*, and obelisk, or *obelus*. He used the asterisk to add into his 5th column where the Hebrew had words, but they weren't in the Greek. When that happened, he usually

Asterisks and Obelisks

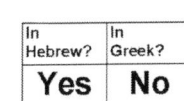

	In Hebrew?	In Greek?
	Yes	**No**

Added Greek to Origen's column to match the Hebrew
(usually from Theodotion).

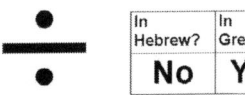

	In Hebrew?	In Greek?
	No	**Yes**

Marked the Greek in Origen's column, that it wasn't in the Hebrew.

Figure 21. Symbols Origen used to show differences in *Hexapla* documents.

---

14) LXX is the Roman numeral for 70. Nobody has ever explained why it's called "70," when it supposedly had 72 translators. But maybe LXX is easier than LXXII.

copied the Hebrew from Theodotion. He used the obelisk to mark in his 5th column where the Greek had words, but they weren't in the Hebrew.

During this big project he wrote commentaries on books of the Bible. He also wrote lessons, or homilies. In them he clearly said that if it is not in the Hebrew, the Alexandrian Greek is wrong. But Origen was not afraid to lie when it was convenient.

So far, Origen's textual theory looks pretty good. His 5th column added in words that were missing from the Greek, and he marked as "spurious" or fake the words that were in the Alexandrian Greek but not in the Hebrew.

But back in Alexandria, some people accused Origen of "fawning on the Jews," and putting down the Alexandrian churches' Bible. That got him in trouble, because those proto-Catholics thought he was abandoning the Old Testament mixed with Apocrypha that they used. The Hebrew didn't have the Apocrypha. So if they went by the Hebrew, they'd have to abandon the Apocrypha and all sorts of other changed texts in their Alexandrian Bible.

They accused Origen of being a traitor to their religion. They were basically right, but Origen couldn't tell them the truth, or he could be excommunicated from their church.

He got the perfect opportunity to state his lie publicly in the late 230s. A convert, a traveler named Sextus Julius Africanus, wrote to Origen. He was born in or near Jerusalem, and spoke and read Hebrew, Latin and Greek. He figured out that the Alexandrian Old Testament had writings in it that weren't in the Hebrew. So he wrote to Origen about it.

Here's the funny thing. Africanus basically stated

everything that Origen already knew. The extra books of the Apocrypha ***didn't*** belong in the Bible, because they weren't in the Hebrew scriptures. They were never accepted as scripture by the Hebrews. But Origen saw an opportunity to clear his name as a "Jew lover."

So Origen wrote back to Julius Africanus. He didn't admit that Africanus was right. Instead, he wrote the ***opposite*** of everything he wrote in his commentaries and homilies. He ***lied his head off!***[15] Origen didn't admit that the Hebrew was correct, refusing the folktales of the Apocrypha from being included as scripture. Instead, Origen said the ancient Jewish elders ***hid*** the truth of these extra stories (like the story of Susanna that's added to Daniel), and kept them from being put into the Hebrew Bible, because they supposedly made the Jewish leaders look bad. Origen told Africanus that the Greek Septuagint is the ***true*** Bible, and not the Hebrew, because God Himself gave the Greek to the Christians. So Africanus should believe the Greek, even though it has ***lots*** of words and stories and sections that aren't in the Hebrew![16] And this letter saved his hide with the Alexandrian churches. Roman Catholics still quote from it to this day, to justify the Apocrypha being in their Roman Catholic Bibles.

Really? This is the same Origen who said that God the Son, God the Holy Ghost, and "the scripture," intentionally put lies into the Bible, so only the "more skillful and

---

15) See «The Letter to Africanus: Origen's recantation?» by NRM De Lange of Cambridge, a paper presented to the 7th International Conference on Patristic Studies held in Oxford, 1975, found in *Studia Patristica* Vol. XVI, Part II, ed. by Elizabeth A. Livingstone (Berlin: Akademie Verlag, 1985), pp. 242-247.
16) See "Letter to Africanus" at http://www.newadvent.org/fathers/0414.htm.

inquisitive" could pick out the lies from the truth![17] You just can't trust this guy. He doesn't talk out of two sides of his mouth. He talks out of three at least!

The bottom line is this. Origen's 5th column of the Hexapla, *with or without* the asterisks and obelisks, got copied and spread around as the "true" Greek Old Testament and Apocrypha. And that letter to Africanus sealed the deal. They trusted him. I told you that Origen was popular. "Origen was the origin." It's no different from a popular preacher endorsing the occultic Lamsa Bible or the Message Bible. People follow their leader like happy little sheeple.

Let me sum up. People kept copying Origen's 5th column, because they trusted Origen. But none of the Alexandrians had a consistent way to copy scripture, or to know what ***was*** scripture. They had no set patterns. That is how the Alexandrian text got to where it is today. You cannot get three supposedly scholarly Alexandrian-type Bibles, Alexandrinus, Vaticanus and Sinaiticus, to match each other.

The Greek is nothing compared to the Hebrew. The Jewish scribes lovingly and faithfully made accurate copies of the Hebrew scriptures through the centuries. By the 600s AD, a group called the Masoretes became the custodians and protectors of the text. They believed it to be the very words of God. So they handled it with extreme care. They gave us a super-accurate Old Testament that is absolutely faithful to the Old Testament scriptures.

In later years, people made up their own Hebrew texts, picking and choosing from other languages and documents,

---

17) See *De Principiis* (On First Principles), Book 4, Sections 8-19. For a clear translation, see *The Church Fathers on the Bible*, ed. by Frank Sadowski, SSP (New York: Society of St. Paul, 1987), pp. 121-122.

Origen-al Sin 41

and using them to change the Hebrew.

But there had to be a name for the text that the Masoretes copied. They called it the Masoretic Text. But it wasn't ***their*** text. It was the preserved text, that they faithfully passed on.

The Codex Leningradensis, dated 1008 AD, is an example that we have to this day of the Masoretic Text.

Figure 22. Book containing a facsimile of the Masoretic Text: Leningrad Codex B19a.

This is a photographic facsimile of a Hebrew Codex, dated about 1008 AD. It was kept in a synagogue in Leningrad. It is one of the earliest complete copies of the Masoretic Text still in existence.

Isn't it beautiful?

All those markings that you'll see around the text of the scripture are supplemental notes meant to "lock in" the scripture in the middle of the page, keeping it safely separate from the commentary and notes in the margins. The scripture was carefully written. They counted lines, letters, spaces. Everything had to match up with the previous copy. That is why when you look at the few Dead Sea scrolls that were copied fairly well, even though we have NO idea where they came from (their provenance) or who copied them (their chain of custody), they are almost letter-for-letter identical to each other.

This particular Masoretic Old Testament has a known provenance. We know where it came from. Levitical priests and scribes passed down the texts from generation to generation. By the 600s, the Masoretes focused on keeping up that tradition of preservation. By doing this, they picked up where the Levites and scribes left off.

Finally, in 1008 AD, Samuel ben Jacob went to a synagogue in Cairo, Egypt, and copied the codex, from manuscripts written by Aaron ben Moses ben Asher. This wasn't done by multiple people, as is typically the case. Samuel ben Jacob actually wrote the consonants, the vowels and the Masoretic notes. The back of the codex in my modern photo facsimile adds notes of every smudge, scrape, mark, and bend in the text. It's amazing. It's nothing like the sloppy mess called the Sinaiticus.

You know why there's such a great difference between the Alexandrian Old Testament and the Hebrew? Because the Jewish copyists called Levites, scribes, and Masoretes believed they were handling God's words. They wouldn't even write the name of God until they had washed and prayed. You won't find a Masoretic copy skipping entire sections of scripture, as you find with Sinaiticus and other Alexandrian Greek texts. [18]

They feared God. But I don't think Origen feared God. I don't think the makers of Sinaiticus feared God. But the people who

---

18) See the vlogs, Why You Can't Trust Sinaiticus at https://youtu.be/wKC1fwnmQ6c and Deleted on Purpose? at https://youtu.be/5zaTPcB2bBs

copied God's preserved words feared God.

That's why I trust my King James Bible. And not only does it have a **known history** of coming from manuscripts **by God-fearing people**. It has also been over 400 years tried and tested, and proved through the fire. The faith of millions has been enhanced by it, and by trusting it, they have served God faithfully and will receive their rewards in heaven.

There is a fundamental difference between King James Bible-believing Christians and those who trust the modern versions. The King James people base their **faith** in the words of the King James Bible.

Modern version people base their **doubts** on their Bibles. People like them intimidate you to doubt like they do. They want you to **doubt the King James Bible and believe the doubters**. People like me are giving you reasons **to believe the King James Bible and doubt the doubters**.

After all I present to you, it really is up to **you** to make your choice. Faith or doubt. The choice is yours.

5

Was There a BC Septuagint?

I've had to search my heart and pray to God that I would be objective. Those of you who have watched my videos already know that after 18 years I was convinced that my Amillennial, end-time views were wrong.[19] And you know, as well, that for 30 years I believed Tischendorf was telling the truth before finding out he was a **liar**.[20]

(I'm still going to have to change the next printing of some of my books because of all this.) So you know I was serious when I told God, "Please, show me the truth. *Was there a BC Septuagint?*"

You see, lots of people through the ages have claimed that Jesus read the Septuagint, a Greek Old Testament, and that His apostles did, as well. They say that if Jesus and the apostles trusted the Septuagint, then so should we.

But the Septuagint also includes the Apocrypha, where we find writings in favor of praying (or paying) for the dead, purgatory, committing suicide, an angel of God lying, sorcery and magic. You can read more in Chapter 15 of

---
19) See Vlog 131: End Times View: Changed! Part 1, at https://youtu.be/GIdIXyyIIhs
20) See 149 Is the Sinaiticus Origin a Lie, at https://youtu.be/--3WTeLmZJE

Why They Changed the Bible.[21]

And the Greek Septuagint is also the basis for the Roman Catholic Latin Vulgate, the official Roman Catholic Bible for 1500 years. Think about this. If the evidence backs the Catholic Bible as the real Bible, Apocrypha and all, then this would back their move to create One World Bible, for Catholics, Protestants, Orthodox and Baptists alike.

Figure 23. Previous book written when I began to see how Satan was creating one world Bible.

*The Vatican and United Bible Societies already have One World Hebrew text and One World Greek Text, as well as One World Latin text. Adding the Apocrypha would be the icing on the cake. And the Apocrypha comes only from the Septuagint Greek, not the Hebrew. The Hebrew speakers never accepted **any** of the Apocrypha as scripture.*

So this is actually a **very** important question. Was the Septuagint made before Christ (BC)? If it turned out I was wrong, it would just be one more change in a world of changes. I promised God that I would change whenever I was proved wrong. That's why I've stood for the KJV for the last 17 years, despite my formal training in Bible college, seminary and SIL (Summer Institute of Linguistics).

*So let's deal with the issue squarely. Is there proof of a BC Septuagint? What is the **best evidence** for a BC Septuagint, and*

---

21) Available from Chick Publications, at http://www.chick.com/catalog/books/0220.asp. See also "What's in Your Bible? Apocrypha Part 1 at https://youtu.be/FxNSZ9NtKhY and "What's Wrong with Tobit? Apocrypha Part 2 at https://youtu.be/o4pZwoR-Pbk

is it a mountain of evidence, or a molehill?

First, I had to find the "best evidence." You can't find a lot of versions of the Greek Septuagint around. The main two are Lancelot Brenton's 1851 *Septuagint with Apocrypha: Greek and English*, based, he claimed, mainly upon the Vaticanus and a little of Alexandrinus. The other is the Ralhfs-Hanhart *Septuaginta* from 1935 and updated in 2006, based upon the blending of Sinaiticus, Vaticanus and Alexandrinus.

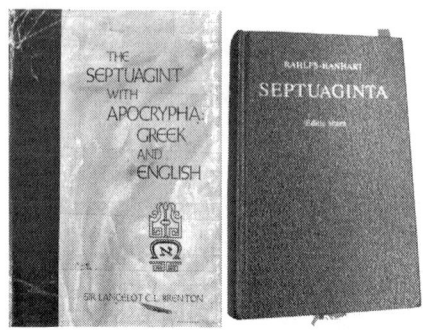

Figure 24. Two main copies of the Septuagint: Brenton's 1851 *Septuagint with Apocrypha* and the 2006 Ralhf's-Hanhart *Septuaginta*.

It also claimed to have some readings from the Hexapla, the 6 Old Testaments in columns done by Origen in the 230s-240s AD. That's all fine. **But that's *all AD*. *None* of that is *BC*.** Only one document, anywhere in history, claims to tell the full story of the creation of the Septuagint. It's called the ***Letter of Aristeas***.

There are two main English translations of the whole

Letter of Aristeas, R. H. Charles' from 1913,[22] and Henry St. John Thackeray's from Cambridge in 1903.[23]

Thackeray also made a 1917 book, "*The Letter of Aristeas, translated with an appendix of ancient evidence on the origin of the Septuagint.*"[24]

That sounds like "best evidence" to me! So let's start there.

---

22) *The Letter of Aristeas*, edited by R.H. Charles (Oxford: The Clarendon Press, 1913).
23) «Translation of the Letter of Aristeas» by Henry St. John Thackeray, in *The Jewish Quarterly Review* (April, 1903), pp. 337-391.
24) *The Letter of Aristeas, translated with an appendix of ancient evidence on the origin of the Septuagint*, by Henry St. John Thackeray (NY: Society for Promoting Christian Knowledge, 1917).

6

Examining the Witnesses of a BC Septuagint

I've wondered for years if there was anything else available to testify to this BC Septuagint. I, and probably you, have *assumed* so much, for so long. It's like when you go into any class, from elementary school to college. The teacher says, "When did the dinosaurs roam the earth?"

Figure 25. Tyrannosaurus Rex.

And they'll say, "Millions of years ago." It's rote memory. It doesn't mean it's true. Everybody just assumes it is.

It was the same in Bible college. The teacher could ask, "When was the Septuagint written?" And we'd say, "*285 BC.*" My wife, Deborah, remembers it. You probably do too, if you went to Bible college or had one of those scholarly Sunday school teachers. Again, we *assumed* it was true. That doesn't mean it was. Nobody actually checked it.

So let's do that now. But we can save the discussion of the actual Letter of Aristeas for afterward.

*Let's talk about the other **supposed** testimonies for a BC*

Septuagint. The best list comes from Thackeray's Appendix, entitled "The Evidence of Some Ancient Jewish and Christian Writers on the Origin of the Septuagint Version." First are the rabbinic Jewish writings.

Rabbinic Jewish Writings

Thackeray's first witness is the *Megillath Taanith*, The *"Roll of Fasting,"* written between 41-70 AD, **three centuries after the supposed Septuagint,** during the revolution of the Zealots.[25]

Figure 26. A modern copy of the Megillath Taanith, the "Roll of Fasting."

It says "On the eighth (or 7th) day of Tebeth (December - January) the Law was written in Greek" (this could simply mean that they wrote out the Hebrew words with Greek letters, not Hebrew letters) "in the days of King Tolmai (Ptolemy), and 'the darkness' (like in Exodus 10:21) came upon the world for three days."[26] That's an interesting quote, but it doesn't tell much.

---

25) It had to be written after "Caligula's plot to introduce an idol into the Temple and the abrogation of his decree upon the timely murder of the Emperor. These events took place in the years 39-41 CE, and the Scroll must have been written after that date.» See *Megillat Taanit* by Professor Vered Noam (digitized 8/10/2006). The Jewish victories listed make it most likely that the scroll was created between 41 and 70 AD.
26) See *The Letter of Aristeas* (1917), p. 89.

List of the Ptolemies

(comparing H St. J Thackeray's list with others)

	B.C.
Ptolemy I, Soter	305-285
Ptolemy II, Philadelphus	285-247
Ptolemy III, Euergetes	247-222
Ptolemy IV, Philopator	222-205
Ptolemy V, Epiphanes	205-182
Ptolemy VI, Eupator	182
Ptolemy VII, Philometor	182-146
Ptolemy VIII, Philopator Neos	146
Ptolemy IX, Euergetes II or Physkon	146-117
Cleopatra III and her sons-	}
Ptolemy X, Philometor II or Soter II or	}
Lathyrus, and	}
Ptolemy XI, Alexander	} all 117-81
Berenike III and	}
Ptolemy XII, Alexander II	} all 81
Ptolemy XIII, Auletes	81-52
Cleopatra VII Philopator,	51-30
her brother/husband Ptolemy XIV	47-44
and her (and Julius's) son Caesarion	44-30

Figure 27. List of all the Ptolemies, over 275 years.

First, which ruler named Ptolemy? Starting with Alexander the Great's General Ptolemy, there were no less than **15 Ptolemies**, 14 of which (plus 7 queens) ruled over Egypt between 305 and 30 BC.

Second, was it started, finished, or all done on the 8th of Tebeth? It doesn't say.

Third, was it translated from Hebrew to Greek, or was it just Hebrew words written in Greek letters —transliterated?

Fourth, where did the story of darkness upon the world for three days come from? We have no such story anywhere else in the world. It would be rather obvious, if it happened.

Somebody would have recorded it.

So I don't trust this story, at all. It sounds like a folktale, not solid evidence. Witness number one is excused.

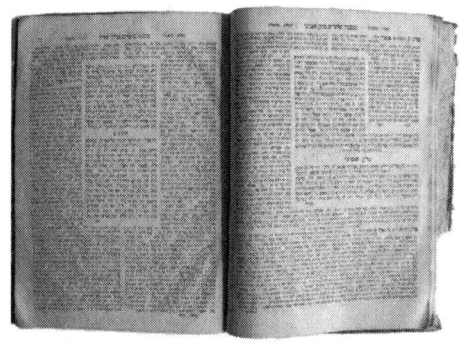

Figure 28. Pages of Masseketh Sopherim, the "Tractate of the Scribes."

Thackeray's second witness is the Masseketh Sopherim, *the "Tractate of the Scribes."* It is a document written in the 700s AD, **almost *1,000 years after the supposed Septuagint*.** Here are excerpts of Part 1, Section 8: "It happened once that *five* **elders** wrote the Law in Greek" (which could mean Hebrew words written in Greek characters) for one of those 15 Ptolemies; "and that day was a hard day for Israel, like the day on which Israel made the *golden calf*...." That means they claimed that they "wrote the Law in Greek," and that it was ***a bad thing.***

Then it basically says that, on another occasion, whichever Ptolemy this allegedly was, put 70 Hebrew elders in 70 cells (private rooms) without telling them why. Then he said, "Write me out the Law of Moses your master." Then all of them were "of one mind" and wrote out the Law, evidently without their own copy of the Hebrew Law, "but they altered 13 passages." Then it lists the passages in detail: 7 in Genesis, 3 in Exodus, 1 in Numbers, and 3 in Deuteronomy... which is weird, because that adds up to 14, not 13.

Going on, **Masseketh Sopherim** also says that the Hebrew names for God in that scroll were all written in gold letters. But it says the wise men replied, "Put it away."

Figure 29. The Cairo, Egypt, geniza (storage room).

They commanded that the scroll be stuck into a *geniza*, a storage room, because the gold letters made it unfit to use in a synagogue.

So now we have a different story. We **still** don't know *which* Ptolemy supposedly ordered the Law to be written. And it says only **70** elders, not 72, like in Aristeas, as you will see. And it claims they all wrote ***the same exact words*** in their private cells, even in the 13 verses (or 14) where they disagreed with the Hebrew... without even one Hebrew text in their possession. Remember, according to this account, the king ***didn't say why*** he was putting them in separate cells, so they had no way to prepare for this.

Masseketh Sopherim also says that just *the names of God* were written in gold, but, guess what? The Letter of Aristeas, Section 176 says the whole **scroll** was written in gold![27] So that testimony doesn't match, either.

I don't trust this account. Neither did the Jewish scholars, it turns out. In modern, printed copies of the Babylonian Talmud, the Masseketh Sopherim is stuck in another section, as an Addendum at the end of the book, apart from the accepted ancient Talmudic writings. They knew it blended in 8th century AD traditions. So they sidelined it in a separate place.

Witness number two is excused.

Thackeray's third witness is the Jerusalem or Palestinian Talmud, 350-400 AD, over *600 years after the supposed Septuagint was made.*

Figure 30. Pages from the Jerusalem Talmud.

This account is found in Megilla I. 71 d (at the bottom). The Jerusalem Talmud account says pretty much the same as the Masseketh Sopherim.[28] So you can't trust this story, either. It has the same problems I just listed. Witness number three is excused.

---

27) See *The Letter of Aristeas* (1917), pp. 89-93.
28) See *The Letter of Aristeas* (1917), p. 93.

Figure 31. Babylonian Talmud.

Thackeray's fourth witness is the Babylonian Talmud, Talmud Bavli, from around 499 AD, *almost 800 years after the supposed Septuagint was made.*

This account is found in Megilla 9a. It matches the story of the Masseketh Sopherim, but changed "seventy" elders to "seventy-two," agreeing with the *Letter of Aristeas*. And it adds the declaration that it was not permitted to translate the Hebrew into *any other language* than Greek. And it had some other differences.[29] So it corrected one part of the "Septuagint story," but the rest of the sections have the same errors. Witness number four is excused.

That's all the witnesses from Rabbinic Judaism, listed in Thackeray's Appendix. *None* of them passes the test. Now for the Hellenistic Greek Jewish writings.

Hellenistic Greek Jewish Writings

Figure 32. Coin image of Aristobulus of Paneas.

---

29) See *The Letter of Aristeas* (1917), pp. 93-95.

Figure 33. Scholars say Aristobulus should be called Pseudo-Aristobulus.

Thackeray's fifth witness is the letter of Aristobulus of Paneas. It was supposedly written around 186-145 BC, ***100 years after the supposed Septuagint,*** because it is addressed to King Ptolemy VII Philometor during his reign. However, so many scholars have disputed this letter that they actually call it Pseudo (fake) Aristobulus.

The only one who claimed the letter even existed was Eusebius of Caesarea in the 300s AD in his *Preparation for the Gospel*. It took me a while to track this one down. I verified the wording in a 1903 translation by E.H. Gifford.[30]

The letter of Pseudo-Aristobulus claims that Plato, who lived in the 300s BC, was a follower of the Laws of Moses and "studied all their details." "But," he said, "the complete **translation** of the Law and all its contents was made under king Ptolemy Philadelphus ... who displayed the greatest zeal, while Demetrius of Phalerum busied himself with the necessary arrangements."[31]

Anybody who reads Plato knows full well that Plato ***did not*** follow the Laws of Moses.

---

30) *Praeparatio Evangelica* (Preparation for the Gospel) by Eusebius of Caesarea, translated by E.H. Gifford (1903). Text transcribed by Roger Pearse. See Chapter 13, Section 12. Found at http://www.tertullian.org/fathers/index.htm.
31) See *The Letter of Aristeas* (1917), p. 96.

Figure 34. Although their images are strikingly similar, Plato certainly did not follow the Laws of Moses.

That's just bogus. And the fact that so many scholars don't believe for a minute that this document is real, pretty much settles it. Besides, again, we only find this letter in Eusebius of Caesarea's writings *in the 300s AD*, and Eusebius had a personal, vested interest in promoting Origen, plus the Septuagint with the Apocrypha, that Eusebius copied from Origen's 5th column of the Hexapla, in the city of Caesarea Maritima, where the Hexapla was located. And this same Eusebius also became lapdog to Emperor Constantine, who pushed Origen and his corrupted Greek Bible.

Witness number five is excused.

Figure 35. Philo of Alexandria, by André Thevet (1584).

Thackeray's sixth witness is Philo of Alexandria, 25 BC-50 AD. He was a Hellenistic Jew who lived in Alexandria, Egypt. He was born into wealth and society, educated in Greek and Roman and Egyptian, as well as Jewish, culture. He believed that the scriptures cannot be understood literally. He started up the "allegorical" (non-literal) method of understanding the Bible that Origen later copied. Philo said God was too marvelous and complex to take Him literally. So, of course, Philo could *not* take God's words of scripture, literally, either.

Figure 36. King Ptolemy II Philadelphus.

Philo's story of the Septuagint, found in ***On the Life of Moses***, Part 2, Sections 5-7, is the most complex one yet. Here are some highlights: First, he waxed eloquent, saying that King Ptolemy II Philadelphus (who reigned from 285-247 BC) was the greatest of all the Ptolemies. Philadelphus had such a "passionate desire" for the Laws of Moses that he sent ambassadors to the high priest and king of Judea, who was the same guy. So the high priest/king found Hebrews trained in Hellenic Greek learning, as well as Hebrew.[32] Then Philadelphus made feasts and asked them philosophical questions.[33] They passed all these tests with flying colors. So Philadelphus found the purest and cleanest undiseased location in the land, the island of Pharos, for them to live and commune with God while they translated.

Here's how Philo described the translation:

"In secret they sat, with none present save the elements

---

32) This matches up with Aristeas, section 121, though Philo here doesn't tell how many there were.
33) This compares to Aristeas, sections 187-293.

of nature, earth, water, air, heaven, whose origin it was their first task to expound (for the cosmogony [origin of the universe] holds the first place in our laws [meaning Genesis 1-2]); and, as men possessed, they produced not divers interpretations, but all alike used the same words and phrases, as though some invisible prompter whispered in the ears of each."

Then he said that they exactly defined every Hebrew word with its corresponding Greek term. And when people read both the Hebrew and the Greek, "they call those men not translators but ***priests*** of the mysteries and ***prophets***, to whom it was vouchsafed with sincerity of mind to enter into the spotlessly pure spirit of Moses."[34]

Figure 37. Huge light house built on the tiny Pharos Island.

---

34) Emphasis mine.

Then Philo claimed there was a yearly festival on Pharos Island to thank God for the Greek translation. So what do we make of this testimony?

First of all, Philo was *not* a Bible believer.

Second, he claimed that the Jewish high priest was also the king. Based on the dates, that would mean either the high priest Onias I, who was high priest until 280 BC, or his son Simon the Just, who was high priest from 280-260 BC. But neither high priest was called or treated as a king. (Remember those names when we come to the *Letter of Aristeas*.)

Third, how expert in Greek culture could the Hebrew translators of the story have been, who had spent their entire existence keeping separate from pagans?

Fourth, who would have taught Jewish people Greek philosophy in Israel in the 280s BC? And what Jews in Israel would have welcomed it?

Fifth, how believable is it that *every* translator, who worked in secret, translated all five books of Moses —Genesis, Exodus, Leviticus, Numbers and Deuteronomy, with the *exact same Greek words?* Or that every one of them had **memorized all 187 chapters of those five books?** And calling them "priests of the mysteries" and "prophets"? ***Really?*** That assumes direct, divine inspiration on every person, simultaneously.

Sixth, there is nobody else who verified a yearly festival out on the isle of Pharos, which means "lighthouse," where the famous 400 foot tall lighthouse of Alexandria stood for 1500 years, constructed starting around 280 BC. And you can bet if there were such a festival on that small island, it would be pretty exclusive, with a limited guest list. And even if there were one in Philo's day, you couldn't know when they started doing it. We have no records. This story is absolutely unverifiable.

Without corroborating evidence, it seems like something that was added to make the story sound legitimate. I could go on. But Philo is saying *too many unbelievable things*. Either someone gave this bogus story to Philo, or Philo made it up himself. Either way, I'm setting aside, but not excusing, witness number six. I will recall him later.

Thackeray's seventh witness is Flavius Josephus, who lived from 37 to about 100 AD, *over 300 years after the supposed Septuagint was made.*

Figure 38. Flavius Josephus.

In 37 AD he was born Joseph ben Matthias, son of a Levite priest. He was well-educated and respected among the Jewish people. He bounced around, from hermit's disciple to Pharisee to negotiator before Nero to free some priests. Then in 66 AD he objected to the Jewish rebellion against Rome. But then he joined the resistance, raised an army, fortified cities… until the next year, 67, where he retreated and then surrendered.

Though he was imprisoned, he became friends with Commander Vespasian, who two years later in 69 AD became emperor. Then Josephus served under Vespasian's son Titus, urging his fellow Jews to surrender to Rome. They didn't.

Figure 39. Emperor Vespasian.   **Figure 40. Emperor Titus.**

In 70 AD Jerusalem was destroyed. But Titus liked Josephus, and took him back to Rome. In 79 AD, Titus became the next emperor. Josephus became his client, got great pay, became a citizen and adopted the emperor's family name, Flavius. He was set for life.

Now, as *Flavius* Josephus, he began writing history books, in a manner pleasing to the Romans. What seems most likely is that Josephus got a lot of information from other people's books, and even remembered stories he was told, and then put them all together into a history of Biblical times and the Jewish people.

You can see how Josephus used other people's stories in his version of the *Letter of Aristeas*. The *Letter* is found in his *Antiquities of the Jews*, Book 12, Chapter 2. Josephus literally took the *Letter of Aristeas*, and paraphrased 100 of the 322 sections. Where *Aristeas* says "I," Josephus put "he." He removed the sections where Aristeas talked to his brother, the list of translators, descriptions of Jerusalem and the philosophical questions the king asked. But this is key: he didn't say anything that disagreed with *Aristeas* at all.

In fact, in 12:2:12, Josephus said you can check the book of Aristeas for more information! Everything Josephus wrote matches the *Letter of Aristeas* as we have it. Josephus doesn't give us anything new, at all. The only thing he ***does*** show is that by 93 AD, the *Letter of Aristeas* was already written and circulating in Rome.

I'll deal with the rest when I go over the Letter of Aristeas. So witness number seven is excused. That's the end of the Hellenistic Greek Jewish writings. And there is still no real evidence to consider. No one has proven the existence of a BC Septuagint. Now for the so-called "Christian" witnesses.

7

The 'Christian' Witnesses.

Figure 41. Justin Martyr, by Andre Thevet (1584).

Thackeray's eighth witness is Justin Martyr, AD 100-165, over *400 years after the supposed Septuagint was made.* He wrote in his *First Apology*, Chapter 31, a story that has so many important changed details, you have to hear it yourself:

"There were, then, among the Jews certain men who were prophets of God, through whom the prophetic Spirit published beforehand things that were to come to pass, ere ever they happened."[35]

---

35) Thackeray was missing the first sentence of the story. I found it in *The Apostolic Fathers, with Justin Martyr and Irenaeus, American Edition* by A Cleveland Coxe, DD. (1885).

"Now when Ptolemy, the king of the Egyptians, was forming a library and endeavoured to make a collection of all men's writings, he heard tell, among the rest, of these prophecies, and sent to Herod, who was then king of the Jews, with a request that the books of the prophecies might be transmitted to him. And King Herod sent them, written in their native Hebrew tongue of which I have spoken. But, since the Egyptians were unacquainted with the things written therein, he sent yet again and requested him [Herod] to dispatch men to render them into the Greek language. This was done and the books remained with the Egyptians and are there to this day."[36]

This one took me by surprise. Justin is a saint to Roman Catholics. But this was a big mistake, or a bald-faced lie. First, Justin wasn't referring to Ptolemy II Philadelphus. The only one alive during the reign of King Herod was Ptolemy XV, Caesarion, son of Julius Caesar and Cleopatra the VII!

And how could Justin talk about Caesarion as king? He was "king" in name only. Cleopatra ruled as Queen. Caesarion was only 10-17 years old during Herod's reign, which began in 37 BC.

Figure 42. Ptolemy XV Caesarion.   **Figure 43. Cleopatra VII, his mother.**

---

36) See *The Letter of Aristeas* (1917), pp. 101-102.

Caesarion and Cleopatra both died in 30 BC. So they only had those 7 years in common to arrange for the Septuagint to be translated, if Justin's story were true.

Besides, the library of Alexandria had been around since the late 200s BC, started by Ptolemy I Soter. No way was the 15th Ptolemy, Caesarion, just "forming a library."

And in this version of the story Justin said it was the ***prophecies***, not the Law, that Ptolemy wanted translated. Justin **rewrote the story** to fit his argument about Hebrew prophecies, it seems. There is nothing accurate about it. But let's give Justin the benefit of the doubt.

What if it was a case of mistaken identity? In 36 BC, Cleopatra had a son with Marc Antony, her third child with him. You know what she named him? ***Ptolemy Philadelphus!*** But Egypt was taken over by Rome before ***this*** Ptolemy Philadelphus turned six years old.

You don't suppose that Justin Martyr thought Cleopatra's *baby* was the Ptolemy Philadelphus of the Septuagint story, do you? If so, he ***really*** got his wires crossed!

I was taught that Justin Martyr was a reliable Christian witness. But now I am stuck with three possibilities: either he got his history book from the bargain bin; he completely changed the story to suit his apologetic lesson; or he mistook a baby in 36 BC with the adult 2nd Ptolemy from 250 years earlier.

Regardless, Justin didn't verify the facts. His account is completely unhelpful. His testimony is, to say the least, not reliable. Witness number eight is excused .

That was the real Justin. But there's also a fake one, **Thackeray's ninth witness, Pseudo-Justin.**

The 'Christian' Witnesses.

Figure 44. The completely unknown Pseudo-Justin.

We have no idea who wrote in Justin's name or exactly when. Obviously it was sometime during or after Justin's life, so at least *400 years after the Septuagint was supposedly written.*

Let me just sum up the story from Pseudo-Justin's writing, *Exhortation to the Greeks*, Part 13.

First, in this story, Ptolemy asked for *70* wise men, not *72*.

Second, he had the 70 Hebrew translators stay on the island "where the Pharos (lighthouse) *was built.*" But the Pharos wasn't finished until years into Philadelphus' reign or else after he died, around 247 BC.

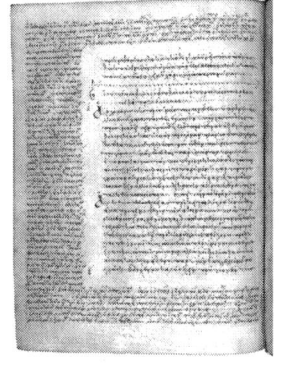

Figure 45. Pseudo-Justin's Exhortation to the Greeks, p. 1. From Bibliotheque nationale de France, gallica.bnf.fr

Third, this *fake* Justin then claimed, "These things which we declare unto you, men of Greece, are no myths nor fictitious history. We ourselves have been in Alexandria and have seen the traces, still preserved, of the cells in the island of Pharos, and have heard this story which we tell you from the inhabitants, who have had it handed down as a tradition of their country. You may learn it from others also, and chiefly from those wise and distinguished men who have written of it, Philo and Josephus, but there are many others besides."[37]

Philo and Josephus were both wrong. Calling them "wise and distinguished" doesn't make their story any more accurate. "**We** declare to you?" *Who's "we"*? We don't even know **who wrote this**. The author lied about his name, saying he was Justin. How could we believe anything else he wrote? So witness number nine is excused.

Thackeray's 10th witness is the famous, often quoted, Irenaeus.

He wrote from 180-202 AD, over *450 years after the Septuagint was supposedly created*. He declared that he had learned from people who had heard from John and the other apostles. But amazingly, none of those early church people mentioned Irenaeus in *their* writings.

Figure 46. Irenaeus of Lyons.

So we have to *trust him* without *any* evidence.

Irenaeus claimed *all* the apostles stated Jesus was *40-50*

---

37) See *The Letter of Aristeas* (1917), pp. 102-103.

years old when He was crucified.[38] But it is clear that Jesus was *really* about *34*. You can see this from the dates of the rulers in Luke and the Passovers and age of the Temple in John. And other early church events show this clearly. Irenaeus is deceived, deceiving, or both.[39]

Irenaeus is also credited as the first person to justify infant baptism. If true, Irenaeus *might* have triggered people into removing Acts 8:37, that says you may be baptized, if you *first* believe in Christ with all your heart. And, of course, a baby can't do that. So they had to either change the doctrine to match the scripture, or remove the scripture. And you know which they did.

It's possible that *someone* he talked to *might* have heard John in an Ephesus church service before he died. But again, there is **no** evidence from **any** source that Irenaeus got **any** of his information from them, or who "they" would be.

It's hard to believe that anyone who paid attention to the apostles would say such inaccurate things as Irenaeus claimed. And there is no way to check up on anything Irenaeus claimed that he heard. I don't see any compelling reason to believe what he wrote. Let's face it. I don't trust the guy.

His Septuagint legend is found in *Against Heresies*, III. xxi. 2, sections 3-4. In his story it was the 1st Ptolemy, Ptolemy I Soter, and not Ptolemy II Philadelphus, who ordered the Alexandrian library built and arranged for the Hebrew and Greek language and culture-knowing Hebrews to come to Alexandria.

---

38) See *Against Heresies*, Book 2, Chapter 22, paragraphs 5-6.
39) See 2 Timothy 3:13.

Irenaeus is the only guy in history to move the story back so far, from the son, Ptolemy II, to the dad, Ptolemy I.

Irenaeus comes across as an unreliable historian at best, and a liar, at worst. Witness number 10 is excused.

Thackeray's 11th witness is Clement of Alexandria, who lived about 150 to about 215 AD, close to *500 years after the Septuagint was supposedly made.*

Figure 47. Clement of Alexandria, by Andre Thevet (1584).

He was an instructor of the school of Alexandria before Origen. Origen was the guy I told you about in Chapter 4, "Origen-al Sin," who wrote that it was okay to lie to people if he didn't feel they were "worthy" of his secrets.

Clement's story, from *Stromateis* I, sections 148-149, was a blend of the stories from Pseudo (fake) Aristobulus and the unreliable Irenaeus.[40] Then he added a few other doozies.

First, he alleged that either Ptolemy I or II asked the Hebrews to translate "the Scriptures, *both of the Law and of the prophets.*" That's Justin Martyr's story blended in, as well.

Second, he never mentioned again the part about translating the Law. He focused on the Prophets.

Clement wrote that *each* of the **70 elders (not 72)** translated each prophecy, and added the absurd story that they were written in the form of Greek prophecies.

Third, he lied two times. He falsely claimed that the

---
40) This was noted by Thackeray in *The Letter of Aristeas* (1917), p. 104.

scriptures totally *perished* during the Babylonian captivity of Judah (probably between 586-536 BC).

Then to cover for the first lie, he made up a second lie that Esdras (Ezra) "was inspired to *revive and prophesy afresh* all the ancient scriptures," literally from **nothing**!

Figure 48. Ezra "restoring" the Old Testament by revelation. Based on Codex Amiatinus, Folio 4 Verso (a 7th century AD copy of 6th century Codex Grandior).

*No way! Clement's lie would mean that God's words perished, and that He broke His own promise to preserve His words. I am amazed that Clement **dared** to say this. Do you see why I don't trust these guys? The more you look, the more these proto-Catholic guys stink.*

We can trust the preserved words of God. They *never* perished, and witness number 11, Clement of Alexandria, has *proved himself to be a liar*. He should not be excused. He should be locked up. That's not a *mistake*. That's full-out *perjury*.

Thackeray's 12th witness is Tertullian, who lived from about 155 to around 240 AD, again almost *500 years after the Septuagint was supposedly written*.

Figure 49. Tertullian, by Andre Thevet (1584).

He wrote his version of the story in his *Apology*, part 18. Let's talk about what stands out in his testimony.

First, Tertullian claimed that Philadelphus set Demetrius of Phalerum as the superintendent over the library of Alexandria. He said that Demetrius was "the most eminent ***philologist*** of his time." A philologist studies ancient books, determines if they are authentic and what they mean.

History doesn't back Tertullian's claim that Philadelphus put such trust in Demetrius of Phalerum, to set him over his library. Demetrius, it turns out, voted ***against*** Philadelphus to make his brother, Ptolemy Keraunos, to be ruler instead of Philadelphus! That tends to make enemies.

When Philadelphus finally took the throne, he got his revenge by sending Demetrius into exile in the south, in upper Egypt. And shortly after 283 BC, Demetrius died of a snake bite, at the very ***beginning*** of Philadelphus' reign. There is no way that Demetrius of Phalerum was a friend of Philadelphus, and there is no time for all that Demetrius supposedly did, to happen.

The 'Christian' Witnesses.

Second, Tertullian said that the 72 translators were held in high esteem by a philosopher named Menedemus, after they answered all the king's questions. But Menedemus lived far away in Eretria, Greece and was *never* said to have visited Alexandria, Egypt, or to have left Greece in his lifetime. But it is very likely that his *writings* were in the library at Alexandria, for whoever made this stuff up to get the idea to include him in the story.

Figure 50. Anatolius of Laodicea.

And **third**, he claimed that the libraries of Ptolemy are still shown in the Serapeum (a branch library in the temple of Serapis) with the actual Hebrew documents that were used by the translators. We can't verify that, since the entire Alexandrian library, including the Serapeum, was destroyed in 391 AD. So 2 out of 3 claims we know for sure are wrong. That makes Tertullian's testimony unreliable. Witness number 12, Tertullian, is excused.

Thackeray's 13th witness is a Catholic saint named Anatolius of Laodicea, who lived from the early 200s to 283 AD, over *500 years after the Septuagint was supposedly made.* He grew up in Alexandria, Egypt in the time of Origen, ran an Aristotelian school, and wrote 10 books on mathematics. Only fragments of them survive today.

He wrote *Canons Concerning the Passover* (the Paschal Canon), and was quoted by Eusebius in *Ecclesiastical History* VII. 32. It's so short I can give you the whole quote.

"The famous Aristobulus, who was enrolled among the Seventy who translated the holy and divine Scriptures of the Hebrews for Ptolemy Philadelphus and his father; he also addressed to those same kings books in which he expounded the meaning of the Mosaic law."[41]

There are two things clearly wrong here.

First, "the famous Aristobulus" is really ***Pseudo***-Aristobulus. His letter was a fake, as you saw.

Second, no account *anywhere* claimed Aristobulus was "enrolled among the Seventy" translators. Even the *fake* story was about a guy (Aristobulus) who was telling about an event that happened over 100 years earlier.

Just because you are smart in math, geometry, physics, astronomy, rhetoric and dialectic, like Anatolius, doesn't mean you are good at history. Witness number 13 is excused.

Thackeray's 14th witness is none other than Eusebius of Caesarea himself.

He lived from 263-339 AD. He was greatly influenced by Julius Africanus. Remember, Africanus had been convinced by the letter from Origen that the Greek Septuagint was from God, after all, even though it *added* all sorts of *extra* words that *weren't* in the Hebrew and was *missing* all sorts of words that *were* in the Hebrew.

Figure 51. Eusebius of Caesarea, by Andre Thevet (1584).

---

41) See *The Letter of Aristeas* (1917), p. 106.

The 'Christian' Witnesses. 75

*Most importantly, the Septuagint included the Apocrypha, which was **never** in the Hebrew Bible.*

Eusebius was the main defender of the BC Septuagint story. Yet he is the ***only*** source of a number of the questionable quotes I've given to you so far, in support of a BC Septuagint.

So let me give you the highlights of what Eusebius wrote about the origin of the Greek Old Testament. He wrote about this in *Preparation for the Gospel*, Book VIII, Chapter 1. It can be found at tertullian.org, along with other writings that are difficult to find, but now made available because of modern technology.

Eusebius claimed that God wanted the prophecies of the Saviour to be in public libraries, accurately translated, before He came to earth. So, Eusebius wrote, "God put it into the mind of King Ptolemy to accomplish this…"[42]

Eusebius said that the Hebrew translation into Greek was "dispensed by *divine providence* and executed by men who for wisdom and learning in their country's lore were held in high repute by their nation." After this, Eusebius simply summarized parts of the Letter of Aristeas in his Book VIII, Chapters 2-5.

It's easy to **justify a legend by** saying "**God** made it happen." But first you have to prove it actually happened at all. It doesn't **become** true all of a sudden, just because someone says it helps his faith. That is a diversion from the question of whether the event actually happened.

---

42) See *Praeparatio Evangelica (Preparation for the Gospel)* by Eusebius of Caesarea, translated by E.H. Gifford (1903), Book 8, Chapter 1.

Figure 52. Forms of the mother goddess Tonantzin.

Some say that **God** made the Virgin Mary goddess appear on the hill of Tepeyac, Mexico, where the mother goddess, Tonantzin was worshipped. They can say it changed their lives for the better. But it doesn't mean that the legend of the Lady of Guadalupe is suddenly a historical event, which no one even heard of until about 118 years after it supposedly happened.

Figure 53. Nuestra Señora de Guadalupe.

In the same way, Eusebius doesn't get a pass for saying that "God put in King Ptolemy's mind to make a Greek Old Testament." First, you'd have to be able to prove that it happened. Then you'd have to be a prophet, to know God's mind. Eusebius failed on both counts.

Quoting other people, who also didn't prove the existence of a BC Septuagint, doesn't cut it, even if he quotes a lot of them. So witness number 14 is excused.

Thackeray's 15th witness is John Chrysostom, who lived from 349-407 AD, over ***650 years after the Septuagint was supposedly made.*** The people called him Chrysostom. It means "Golden Mouth." But I keep thinking of the rock group Smash Mouth, because, seriously, he looks like a rock star in this picture.

Figure 54. John Chrysostom.

This "golden mouth" spoke at the "Golden" church of Antioch.[43] When people heard he was in an area, they wanted him to be the main speaker. So his mouth made him very popular. It also got him in a lot of trouble. On the good side, he told about the evils of focusing on outward appearance and expensive things, but ignoring the poor. Of course, that got one rich lady named Aelia Eudoxia, wife of Emperor Arcadius, all upset. She took it personally and held it against him.

But Chrysostom also got upset at Christians who joined with Jews in their feasts. He preached against that in 8 homilies "Against the Jews."[44] That's where his mouth crossed the line. He launched into a tirade against Jewish people. It was supposed to be a sermon against Judaizers, people who try to get Christians under the Law of Moses.[45]

But he got carried away. He started calling the Jewish people as a whole "the slayers of Christ." In Homily 6 of 8 Chrysostom said this:

"For the martyrs have a special hatred for the Jews, since

---

43) It was called the *Domus Aurea* ("Golden House").
44) Available at www.tertullian.org
45) See, for instance, Acts 15:10-11 and Colossians 2:16-17.

the Jews crucified him for whom they have a special love. The Jews said: 'His blood be on us and on our children.' The martyrs poured out their own blood for ***him whom the Jews had slain.***"[46]

Then he ***denied*** that the Jewish people will ***ever*** have the Temple back again. I don't know how he could stand in the place of God and say something like that. Then he called them ***murderers*** and ***devilish***, because they tried to keep the festivals, even though they didn't have a Temple in Jerusalem. Some say that these 8 sermons caused a world of anguish for the Jewish people, and were the basis for a lot of the Jewish persecution by Roman Catholics that followed, even to this day.

Figure 55. Two-faced Origen.

Chrysostom also really liked two-faced Origen. He proved it by taking in 4 Origenist monks, called the "Tall Brothers," who fled Theophilus, the patriarch of Alexandria, to avoid being disciplined by him. That was a no-no. And that got him banished from Constantinople (with Aelia Eudoxia's help). But he was *so popular* that the people threatened to burn down the royal palace if they didn't get Chrysostom back! So he was brought back —for a while.

Now let's read what Chrysostom said about the origin of the Septuagint. This comes from *Homilies on St. Matthew*, V. 2:

"The Seventy may justly be deemed more trustworthy

---

46) Emphasis mine.

The 'Christian' Witnesses.

than the rest of the translators. The others translated after the coming of Christ, continuing to be Jews, and might with justice be suspected of having spoken rather from enmity and of obscuring the prophecies of set purpose. But the Seventy, in that they approached their task *a hundred or more years* before the coming of Christ[47] and were so many, are above all such suspicion, and by reason of their date, their number and their agreement may well deserve the greater credence."[48]

Let's take that apart. First, he talked of "the Seventy," but as you have seen, no one even proved that they existed. Then he says **70**, not **72** translators, as the *Letter of Aristeas* claims. Next, he said only "*a hundred or more years before the coming of Christ*" —over 6 generations of difference between **100** BC and **285** BC!

Then he claimed they could be trusted, because they weren't like the later Jewish people who rejected Christ, whom he suspected of changing the Bible. He didn't trust rejecters of Christ, but he trusted "the Seventy." But how can I put my **trust** in someone who may not have even *existed*?

*The point is this. Even "Saint" John Chrysostom didn't **prove** the existence of a BC Septuagint, at all. He only **assumed** it. So witness number 15 is excused.*

Thackeray's 16th witness is Epiphanius of Salamis on the isle of Cyprus, who lived from about 315 to 403 AD,

---

47) [Thackeray's footnote:] "In his *Homilies on Genesis*, IV. 4, he puts the [LXX] translation under 'a certain King Ptolemy not many years before the coming of Christ.' Other dates mentioned are **230** BC (Pseudo-Athanasius, *Synopsis*), **31** BC (Pseudo-Theodoret), and **301** BC (Nicetas, *Catena on the Psalms*)."
48) See *The Letter of Aristeas* (1917), p. 108. Emphasis mine.

over ***650 years after the Septuagint was supposedly made***.

This picture is of an icon of Epiphanius. That's so ironic, because he spoke against heresies, including the heresy of **making icons!**

Figure 56. Icon of St. Epiphanius. From the Gračanica monastery, Kosovo.

Jerome, the creator of the Roman Catholic Latin Vulgate, had been Epiphanius' buddy since he was in his 20s. He called Epiphanius "Five-tongued," because he could speak in five languages: Hebrew, Syriac, Egyptian, Greek, and Latin.

Epiphanius is best known for two book series: One was called *Against Heresies*, or the *Panarion* (medicine chest), and the other called *On Weights and Measures*,[49] which talks about the Old Testament, measures and weights, and Israel's geography.

On the one hand, the guy *looked* very thorough in his writing. But it turns out that his research wasn't so carefully done. For some of the 80 heresies he wrote about, he relied on hearsay evidence. Someone would say that an event occurred, and Epiphanius just took it as true and wrote strongly against it. You can make big mistakes that way.

Ironically, Epiphanius was ***anti-Origen***. He traced pretty much every heresy to Origen and Origenism. And his teachings influenced Thackeray's last witness, author of the

---

49) There are three places to find Epiphanius' *On Weights and Measures* in English: www.tertullian.org/fathers, transcribed by Roger Pearse in 2005, and the book it came from, found at oi.uchicago.edu when you search for "weights and measures," or at www.archive.org.

The 'Christian' Witnesses.

Roman Catholic Latin Vulgate and his good friend: Jerome. Epiphanius spent years in Egypt with anti-Origen monks. After that, he spent the rest of his life fighting Origen's teaching as he saw it as the root of the 80 heresies of his day.[50]

One of his last battles, in fact, was against "Golden Mouth" ***Chrysostom***, for taking in those four pro-Origen monks who fled Egypt. Epiphanius wished that Chrysostom wouldn't die a bishop. And Chrysostom wished that Epiphanius would not live to arrive home. Believe it or not, ***both curses came true!*** Chrysostom was deposed and exiled as you saw, and Epiphanius died at sea, on the way back home to Cyprus![51]

Even though Epiphanius did a lot of writing, historians agree his research wasn't the best. As I said, many times he trusted ***hearsay*** instead of actual evidence. And it was ironic: even though Epiphanius seemed against everything Origen did, he grew up using Origen's approved Septuagint. So he didn't say anything bad against ***it***, just ***everything else*** Origen stood for!

It was in the misnamed *On Weights and Measures*,[52] sections 3-11, that Epiphanius added a whole bunch of fanciful elements to the Septuagint story that we can find nowhere else. Here's a quick summary:

1. He said the 72 translators, 6 from each of the 12 tribes of Israel, were in 36 cells, two per cell.

---

50) *Epiphanius' Treatise on Weights and Measures, the Syriac Edition*, Ed. by James Elmer Dean (Chicago: University of Chicago Press, 1935), p. vii.
51) See *Epiphanius' Treatise on Weights and Measures* (1935), p. 2.
52) Actually, only ***one part*** of the treatise deals with weights and measures.

2. The cells only had a roof window.

3. All 36 rooms were locked by day.

4. They were provided two youths to give them food, and were given scribes, as well.

5. To every pair, one book of the Bible was given, of every book of the Old Testament used by the Hebrews, plus the apocryphal Wisdom of Solomon and Sirach, the Epistle of Baruch and Epistle of Jeremiah, etc.

6. Every night they would take small boats back to Philadelphus' palace to dine with him.

7. Then they slept in 36 separate bedchambers, so the pairs wouldn't talk with the others.

8. Each day they rotated the books of the Bible and Apocrypha among the 36 pairs. He went into great detail on how they did this.

9. In total, Epiphanius claimed the Old Testament books were translated 36 times, and the "22 [books] that are apocryphal," 36 times.

10. At the end, the king had 36 readers with the 36 duplicates, and one person who read the Hebrew. Each reader read alone, and the others checked their text.

Amazingly, according to Epiphanius, not a ***single*** text was different in a ***single*** word, not even the words that we know were ***added to*** the Hebrew or ***taken from*** the Hebrew!

11. Thus the story goes that in the 7th year of Philadelphus' reign over Egypt (in the 270s BC), the king finally had one copy of the Hebrew scriptures, plus 36 copies of a perfect, Holy Spirit inspired Greek Old Testament, plus 22 books of the Apocrypha.

Perfectly believable, right? ***No way!*** No one had ever

conjured up a fabricated story like this one. He went far beyond the ***Letter of Aristeas*** to spin this yarn. I bet it was a thrilling story to hear around the campfire. The only problem is he's the only guy to ever tell it this way. There's too much ***brand new information*** out of nowhere for a guy to claim to know, who lived over ***600 years*** after the event was supposed to have happened. So witness number 16 is excused.

Henry St. John Thackeray's 17ᵗʰ and final witness was Jerome.

Figure 57. "St. Jerome in His Study." by Pieter Coecke van Aelst the elder (about 1530).

Jerome was the last historical person listed by Thackeray, in his evidence on the origin of the Septuagint. He lived from about 347 to 420 AD, writing over ***650 years after the Septuagint was supposedly made***.

*Jerome is also the **last person** in a chain of events that leads directly to the creation of the Roman Catholic Latin Vulgate. The Vulgate, you see, was translated largely from the Greek*

Septuagint. And the Septuagint contained the Apocrypha that was so useful to Roman Catholic doctrines.

Let's sum up that chain so far:

We start with the story of the Septuagint. Whether it was made BC or AD, we know that there was a Greek text that was in use by about 50 AD, that continued through the 230s until Origen's ***Hexapla***. We don't have any actual copies of the whole text. We just know that it existed, both from translations of parts of it or notes that were made from it.

The Hexapla listed four Greek translations of the Hebrew text, from the most literal to the most "free," Aquila being the most literal, followed by Symmachus, then Theodotion in the loose translation category.

At the same time, the two-faced liar Origen went two different directions. One of them was to critically examine the so-called Septuagint of his day in that giant, multi-volume Hexapla to tell what was **added** in the Septuagint Greek but **not** from the Hebrew text, as well as what was **missing** from the Septuagint Greek but clearly **in** the Hebrew text.

He added the asterisk and obelisk markings, so anyone could tell which was added and which was missing. Then he wrote commentaries and homilies that clearly said this: if it isn't in the Hebrew Old Testament, it isn't really scripture and should be removed.

But Origen also wrote the famous letter to Sextus Julius Africanus, saying the ***opposite***. Origen lied, saying that Jewish leaders removed from the Bible anything that made them look bad. That was why the Apocrypha is not in the Hebrew text, he claimed. But he pretended that God Himself added it to the Septuagint Greek, so POOF! That meant the **added** words were from God. And the words that were removed were not needed, and the supposed 72 translators did all this in perfect harmony, by the Spirit of God.

What hogwash!

So when Origen wrote to his scholar-friends, he said the **Hebrew** text was the true Old Testament scripture. But when he communicated with the churches of Alexandria, he said the Septuagint **Greek** text was the actual scripture. Which one was it? He gave two contradictory answers.

That's the kind of guy Origen was.

Now, since his 20s, Jerome had been best friends with Epiphanius, the Origen-hater. And as I said, Epiphanius claimed all 80 heresies of his day had their origin in Origen. But he said that Origen's Hexapla was wonderful.

So when Jerome was commissioned in 382 AD to make an official Roman Catholic Latin Bible, he had a choice: would he translate the preserved Hebrew text or Origen's corrupted Greek text?

Enter Augustine of Hippo, the famous Catholic you hear about a lot, who later wrote *City of God* and *Confessions*. Augustine loved Origen's Greek text, and he wrote to Jerome that it would divide the Alexandrian churches against Rome if Jerome's Roman Catholic Latin Vulgate didn't use Origen's Greek.

For over 11 years, Augustine *pled* with Jerome in letters, from 394-405 AD, to change back any places that were different from "the Seventy." But Jerome replied that Augustine didn't even have the "Septuagint text." He had ***Origen's*** text from the 5th column of the Hexapla, with all his added markings, the asterisks and obelisks.

This is an important point. Jerome's admitted to Augustine the truth that Catholic churches were not using the so-called Septuagint at all. They were using that 5th column of the *Hexapla*, which was Origen's own modified Greek text. If the churches of the later 200s-300s used Origen's text and not the so-called Septuagint, then we cannot say that any manuscripts dated after the 300s are the Septuagint, either. We have no complete copies of *any* Greek Bible before Origen.

So no one can say with any certainty that Vaticanus or Alexandrinus, which came after Origen, are the so-called Septuagint, either —much less the modern hoax, Codex Sinaiticus.[53]

Figure 58. Jerome and Augustine. "San Agustín con el Escorial en la mano" by Alonso Sánchez Coello, (1580-82), at the Monasterio del Escorial, Madrid.

Jerome basically told Augustine, "If you want a pure Septuagint, you can remove all the places with asterisks, where Origen added in Theodotion's Greek translation of the Hebrew where sections were *missing* in the Septuagint. Jerome hated Theodotion. He called Theodotion "a Jew and a blasphemer,"[54] whose translation Origen should ***never*** have

---

53) See the playlist, "Something Funny About Sinaiticus," at www.youtube.com/c/chicktracts.
54) *See A Select Library of Nicene and Post-Nicene Fathers of the Christian Church* Vol. 1, St. Augustin, Edited by Philip Schaff & Henry Wace (NY: Charles Scribner's Sons, 1907), p. 341.

copied from.

It sounded from their back and forth letters that Jerome was going to make a Latin Bible that matched right up with the Hebrew. That's what my Fuller Seminary professors told me. "Jerome was the first modern text critic," they would say, ignoring Origen's earlier work on the Hexapla. If Jerome had made a Latin text right from the Hebrew and only the Hebrew, that would have been wonderful! But surprise! He didn't!

I have checked numerous experts to find out how Jerome *really* put together his Roman Catholic Latin Vulgate Old Testament. It turns out that the 39 regular Old Testament books were only loosely translated from the Hebrew. But they were clear enough to see he had and used the same Hebrew as we have today. But despite what he wrote to Augustine, he also translated —and added— the non-Hebrew Apocryphal books. He added them in *five different ways*.

1. Jerome employed a Jewish man to translate an Aramaic text of **Tobit** and **Judith** for him and read it to him in Hebrew. Then Jerome paraphrased what the man said to him into Latin.

2. Jerome translated the **additions to Esther** from the Greek Septuagint. But he also translated a second version from a Hebrew translation.

3. Jerome translated the **additions to Daniel** (**Susanna, Song of the Three Young Men**, and **Bel and the Dragon**) from Theodotion's column of the Hexapla. But he also translated a second one from a Hebrew translation.

4. Jerome already had Latin texts for **Baruch**, the **Letter of Jeremiah**, **Wisdom of Solomon**, **Ecclesiasticus** (Sirach), and **1**

and 2 Maccabees.

5. Jerome translated other books into Latin that were neither in the Greek Septuagint nor in Hebrew. They were ***4 Esdras***, the ***Prayer of Manasses*** and the ***Epistle to the Laodiceans***.

So in short, Jerome wrote against the Septuagint, but he translated parts of it and added them to his Bible, anyway. Jerome wrote in his preface to Job, "the Jewish Aquila, Symmachus, and Theodotion, judaising heretics."[55] And yet Jerome's Roman Catholic Latin Old Testament is a blending of all kinds of sources, including ***them!*** I would have thought he would have stuck to his convictions. However, that is not the case.

But there was one more test to perform.

I have tried to check the best copies of Jerome's Roman Catholic Vulgate that I can find. Mine is dated 2007.[56] Here's the question: Did Jerome ***really*** trust the Hebrew for the 39 genuine Old Testament books, like my professors said? Or did he change them? Take a look at two revealing verses.

Genesis 3:15. ***With a single word***, the doctrine was changed. In the real Bible, God said to the serpent:

"And I will put enmity between thee and the woman, and between thy seed and her seed; ***it*** shall bruise thy head, and thou shalt bruise his heel."

"It" refers to the woman's seed, who is Jesus Christ.

But in Jerome's vulgate, it says ***ipsa*** —she! And by "she,"

---

55) *A Select Library of Nicene and Post-Nicene Fathers of the Christian Church*, Vol. 6, St. Jerome, edited by Philip Schaff & Henry Wace (NY: Charles Scribner's Sons, 1912), p. 491.

56) *Biblia Sacra Iuxta Vulgatam Versionem*, 5th Revised Edition, edited by Roger Gryson, (Stuttgart: Deutsche Bibelgesellschaft, 2007).

Jerome meant **Mary**! That's why you see all those pictures and idols of Mary around the world, with her foot on a snake. Because of Jerome —not even the Septuagint has it— Roman Catholics have been taught the lie that Mary is the Queen of Heaven and the co-mediator with Christ, who actually crushes the serpent, conquers the Devil, and brings salvation!

Blasphemy!

And this word, ***ipsa***, from Jerome's Roman Catholic Latin Vulgate, was translated into English as *"she"* in the Douay-Rheims Bible of 1610 that was in use until the Confraternity Bible. Then the New American Bible of 1970, which silently fixed the verse, took its place. But the damage of 1500 years had been done. Today Roman Catholics ***still*** pray to statues and pictures of Mary with her foot on a snake.

What about Psalm 14:3 (13:3 in the Septuagint and Vulgate)? Does Jerome's Latin copy the Hebrew, or does it add Paul's words from Romans 3:13-18? Surprise! Just like the Septuagint, it adds ***all*** of Paul's words. Here it is, Latin Vulgate on the left, Douay-Rheims on the right.

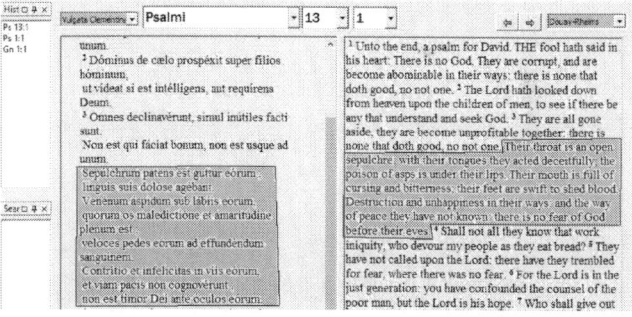

Figure 59. Psalm 13:3 in the Latin Vulgate and Douay-Rheims Bible. (The 2007 Vulgate is identical to the Clementine you see here.)

Did the Roman Catholics say it didn't belong? Look at their commentaries.

Figure 60. Roman Catholic Confraternity Bible (1950, 58, 61).

First, here is the Confraternity Bible.

That was from when they were transitioning the Roman Catholics from the Douay-Rheims to the New American Bible. Look at the note for Psalm 13:3.

"Here many Greek and Latin texts *insert* the Old Testament quotations which were *first* combined in Rom 3, 13-18."

And here is a 1970 New American Bible. It has *the same note*.

Figure 61. Catholic New American Bible (1970).

Remember: from 405 AD to the 1970s, Roman Catholics had an official Bible that *added Paul's words* from Romans 3:13-18 *into* Psalm 14:3. If they were willing to change God's words here, what *else* were they willing to change?

It is clear that Jerome is not trustworthy. On top of **not** fixing Psalm 14:3, he inserted a heresy into Genesis 3:15 to say "she," *Mary*, would bruise Satan's head, indoctrinating generations of Mary worshippers.

Now, finally, let's see what he said about the origin of the Septuagint. This is from Jerome's *Preface to the Pentateuch*:

"I know not who was the first lying author to construct the seventy cells at Alexandria, in which they were separated and yet all wrote the same words, whereas Aristeas, one of the bodyguards of the said Ptolemy, and long after him, Josephus have said nothing of the sort, but write that they were **assembled in a single hall** (Jerome said "basilica") and conferred together,[57] **not that they prophesied**. For it is one thing to be a prophet, another to be an interpreter." [58]

(Jerome seems to have forgotten that "the first lying author" who called "the 70" translators "prophets" was Philo himself, before 50 AD, half a century *before* Josephus!)

And this is from Jerome's *Commentary on Ezekiel*, II. 5 (on Ezekiel 5:12):

"Yet Aristeas and Josephus and the whole Jewish school assert that **only the five books of Moses** were translated by the Seventy."[59]

Did you notice? The two supposedly most scholarly men of their time, Augustine and Jerome, both kept calling the alleged translators of the Septuagint "The Seventy." The *Letter of Aristeas* says **72**, never 70.

Jerome also said it was only Genesis through Deuteronomy that were translated, contradicting his own close friend Epiphanius, who claimed the Septuagint was the entire Old Testament plus "22 apocryphal books."

And despite everything else, after reviewing 650 years of possible evidence, we find that Jerome gave *no evidence* — no actual, verifiable facts. And his story was nothing that we

---

57) See *The Letter of Aristeas*, section 302.
58) See *The Letter of Aristeas* (1917), p. 115. Emphasis mine.
59) See *The Letter of Aristeas* (1917), p. 116. Emphasis mine.

haven't already heard. He is still basing his story off of the *Letter of Aristeas*, like so many others.

So ***none of Thackeray's 17 witnesses*** said anything more than was (or was alleged to be) in the *Letter of Aristeas*. Let's now see what that letter actually says, in its official form.

8

The Letter of Aristeas

To recap, the *Letter of Aristeas* is available in two main translations: R.H. Charles' from 1913, and Henry St. John Thackeray's from 1903. Working from R.H. Charles' copy, the *Letter of Aristeas* in English has, after I removed verse and chapter numbers: 19,407 words. If we were to print it on our press, that would be equal to a 98 page book, not counting formatting, headings, or table of contents.

*So the Letter of Aristeas is not a letter, at all. It's really a **book**! And it's a book of **propaganda**.*

It's supposed to be a letter from a Gentile guy named Aristeas to his brother, Philocrates. But who would write the following to his brother in a letter?

"And I suppose that the thing will seem incredible to those who will read my narrative in the future. But it is unseemly to misrepresent facts which are recorded in the public archives. And it would not be right for me to transgress in such a matter as this. I tell the story just as it happened, conscientiously avoiding any error."[60]

Sounds like he declared his purpose: to set up a supposed "letter," for people "***in the future***" to read. This is exactly

---

60) *The Letter of Aristeas* (1913 translation by RH Charles), sections 296-297.

what a con would do, when setting up a letter and then pretending it is old.

Figure 62. Roman statue of Aristeas (117-138 AD).

"See? It says people will read it in the future. So it **must** be from the past!" Methinks he doth protest too much. **Somebody** is faking his readers out.

And the letter saying the proof is "in the public archives," is another con, since that was supposed to have once been true *in the distant past*. You cannot go back to the past and check. What works is legitimate eyewitness testimony, either of the events, or of the information being in the archives.

Now, if that were all, we could say I'm being too suspicious. But let's find out more about this supposed "letter."

Thackeray noted, "...the letter is not what it professes to be..." and goes on to say that the letter is made to look like "a contemporary record of a Greek who played a prominent part in the actions described..."[61]

First, who is Aristeas? Aristeas claimed to have lived during the reign of the 2nd Ptolemy over Egypt, Philadelphus. Aristeas said that Philadelphus had a great friend named Demetrius of Phalerum, whom he set over his newly-made library of Alexandria. But Philadelphus wanted a copy of the scriptures of the Hebrews for his library. First, he contacted the high priest and got a Hebrew copy. But he

---

61) See *The Letter of Aristeas* translated with an appendix of ancient evidence on the origin of the Septuagint, by Henry St. John Thackeray (New York: The Macmillan Company, 1917), pp. vii-ix

The Letter of Aristeas

couldn't read Hebrew. So he made a deal. He asked for 72 scholars, 6 from each of the 12 tribes of Israel, to come to Alexandria and translate it into Greek. When they came, he asked them many difficult questions of philosophy. The king was so impressed that he gave them an island apart from the people to work. And soon they presented to him a translation of the Hebrew Old Testament scriptures into Greek. That was later called the Septuagint.

But the story has some problems.

Aristeas did not live at the same time as King Ptolemy II Philadelphus. We can see this, because "Aristeas" writes "as though he were looking back over an epoch of a long dynasty of Ptolemies," which we see in sections 28 and 182. In other words, Aristeas wrote as if he were talking about kings of the distant past.

First, Aristeas wrote in section 28: "For all affairs of state **used to be carried out** by means of decrees and with the most painstaking accuracy by **these Egyptian kings**, and nothing was done in a slipshod or haphazard fashion." Aristeas wrote as if he were referring to a line of Egyptian kings. But there had only been one: Philadelphus' dad!

Then from 182: "For this arrangement had been made by the king and it is an arrangement **which you see maintained to-day**." He claims the letter was written during the reign of the 2nd King Ptolemy. But he wrote as if there were a whole string of Ptolemies before him! How many centuries did "Aristeas" live, anyway?

The *Letter of Aristeas* tells of a Demetrius of Phalerum. He is very important to dating the story. So who is Demetrius? He's supposed to be King Ptolemy Philadelphus' confidential friend and set over the newly-created library of Alexandria.

But we know that Demetrius was exiled to northern Egypt, got bitten by a snake, and died about 283 BC. Typically, dead people can't be running a library.

And that's another problem. Epiphanius of Salamis and many modern scholars say the Septuagint was translated in the 7th year of Philadelphus' reign. That would have been about 276 BC, at least 6 years *after* Demetrius died.

Then they quote Aristeas, which says the high priest was **Eleazar**.

Apocrypha: *Ecclesiasticus (Sirach)* 4:1	Josephus: *Antiquities of the Jews* xii, 2, 5 (ca. 94 AD)
37. (not listed)	Onias I
38. Simon I	Simon the Just
39. (not listed)	Eleazar

Figure 63. Jewish high priests, according to Josephus and Old Testament Apocrypha.

After the Babylonian Exile [edit]

- Joshua, son of Jehozadak, ca. 515-490 BC, after the restoration of the Temple
- Joiakim, son of Joshua, ca. 490-470 BC
- Eliashib, son of Joiakim, ca. 470-433 BC
- Joiada, son of Eliashib, ca. 433-410 BC
  (A son married a daughter of Sanballat the Horonite for which he was driven out of the Temple by Nehemiah)
- Johanan, son of Joiada, ca. 410-371 BC
- Jaddua, son of Johanan, ca. 371-320 BC, during the reign of Alexander the Great. Some have identified him as Simeon the Just.

The five descendants of Joshua are mentioned in Nehemiah, chapter 12, 10f. The chronology given above, based on Josephus, however is not undisputed, with some alternatively placing Jaddua during the time of Darius II and some supposing one more Johanan and one more Jaddua in the following time, the latter Jaddua being contemporary of Alexander the Great.

- Onias I, son of Jaddua, ca. 320-280 BC
- Simon I, son of Onias, ca. 280-260 BC
- Eleazar, son of Onias, ca. 260-245 BC

Figure 64. High priests of Israel from Wikipedia, which lists many references for these dates.

But the Hebrews' and historians' lists of high priests don't say that. They say that **Onias I** was high priest until 280 BC. Then **Simon I** was high priest from 280-260 BC. Then **Eleazar**, another son of Onias I, was high priest from 260-245. *Aristeas* would make Eleazar high priest in 276-283, ***16-23 years too early***. Aristeas got his history all mixed up. He just can't seem to get his dates straight.

That's not all. In sections 180-181, Philadelphus supposedly said of the Hebrew translators' arrival, "It happens also that it is the anniversary of my naval victory over Antigonus." No, it wasn't. He confronted Antigonas Gonatas in 260 BC, ***16*** years later, and lost —horribly. He didn't defeat him until 245 BC, ***31*** years later. Aristeas' history is all wrong.

So I ask again, who *is* Aristeas? The picture I showed you earlier was actually a statue of a Greek minor garden deity called Aristeas, because the god Aristeas doesn't actually exist. And I think *this* Aristeas didn't actually exist, either.

Both Thackeray and many Jewish writers that I have read, have agreed that the *Letter of Aristeas* is "Jewish propaganda under a heathen mask." In other words, whoever wrote the *Letter of Aristeas* was a Jewish person, not a Gentile.

I've been chipping away at the Letter all through this book, as you may have noticed. So let me just say, I believe the Letter of Aristeas is a complete fabrication, a fraud, a fiction, and it doesn't even have a grain of truth.

But if I'm right, who could have written it, and why? I'll answer that after we tackle the Dead Sea Scrolls.

9

The Dead Sea Scrolls

Ever since scrolls and 17,000 bits of scrolls were found in caves near the Dead Sea starting in 1946, people have been looking for evidence of ancient Bibles. They have found some astounding things, like scrolls of books of the Old Testament that are virtually identical with the Hebrew Leningrad Codex of 1008 AD, and with other Hebrew Masoretic Texts in the preserved stream.

But some people have been desperate to find a BC Septuagint. Take a look at this:

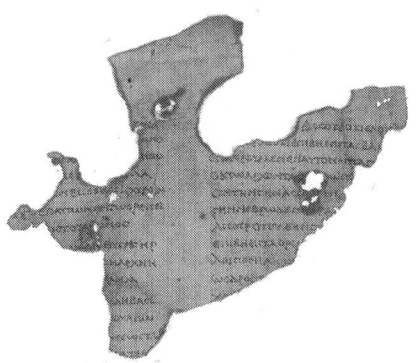

Figure 65. Nahal Hever 8Hev1 to 8Hev XII, parts of Greek Micah 4:6-5:4 and 5:4-6:4.

This is a Nahal Hever Greek text, found in a cave near Hebron.[62]

It has Micah 5:4-6 in the right column.

```
                                                          Column 9
[αυτη ειρηνη] Ασσουρ οτι Ελθη [ει]ς [την γην]                1
[ημω]ν και οτι επιβη επι τας βαρ[εις ημων, και]              2
επεγερουμεν επ' αυτον επτα π[οιμενας και]                    3
οκτω αρχοντας ανθρωπω[ν.] ⁵[και ποιμανου-]                   4
σιν την γην ασσουρ εν ρ[ομφαια και την]                      5
γην νεβρωδ εν παραξ[ιφι, και ρυσεται εξ]                     6
Ασσουρ, οτι ελθη εις τ[ην γην ημων και οτι]                  7
επιβη εις τα ορια [ημων. ⁶Και εσται κατα-]                   8
λοιπον ιακωβ [εν μεσω λαων πολλων]                           9
ως δροσος [παρα 𐤉𐤄𐤅𐤄, ως αρνες επι]                         10
χο[ρτον, ος ουκ υπεμενον ανδρι]                             11
```

[The rest of 5:6b-7:20 missing due to fragmentary scroll]

Figure 66. Nahal Hever Greek Micah 5:4-6 digital text

I decided to take a digital text of the Nahal Hever Greek (above), and compare it to what we call the Septuagint (below). I really gave it the benefit of the doubt. When it had only part of a word that matched, I highlighted those letters.

---

62) Hebron is the city where Abraham and others lived. See Genesis 13:18; 35:27; 37:14.

BGT **Micah 5:4-6**

Actual visible text. (Shaded text matches the Rahlfs Septuaginta):

Ἀσσύριος ἐπέλθῃ
ὑμῶν καὶ ὅταν ἐπιβῇ ἐπὶ τὴν
ἐπεγερθήσονται ἐπ' αὐτὸν ἑπτὰ π
ὀκτὼ δήγματα ἀνθρώπων
σιν τὸν Ἀσσουρ ἐν ρ
γῆν τοῦ Νεβρωδ ἐν τῇ τάφρῳ
Ἀσσουρ ὅταν ἐπέλθῃ ἐπὶ τ
ἐπιβῇ ἐπὶ τὰ ὅρια
ὑπόλειμμα τοῦ Ιακωβ
ὡς δρόσος
ἄγρῳ

[Text not included in the scrap:

[καὶ ἔσται αὕτη εἰρήνη ὅταν
[ἐπὶ τὴν γῆν
[χώραν ὑμῶν καὶ
[οιμένες καὶ
[⁵ καὶ ποιμανοῦ-
[ομφαίᾳ καὶ τὴν
[αὐτῆς καὶ ῥύσεται ἐκ τοῦ
[ἡν γῆν ὑμῶν καὶ ὅταν
[ὑμῶν ⁶ καὶ ἔσται τὸ
[ἐν τοῖς ἔθνεσιν ἐν μέσῳ λαῶν πολλῶν
[παρὰ κυρίου πίπτουσα καὶ ὡς ἄρνες ἐπὶ
[στιν ὅπως μὴ συναχθῇ
[μηδεὶς μηδὲ ὑποστῇ ἐν υἱοῖς ἀνθρώπων

Figure 67.
8Hev XII: Greek Micah 5:4-6 compared to Rahlfs *Septuaginta*.

The gray shows what part of the Nahal Hever matches the *Septuaginta*. We already know this is not the same as the preserved Hebrew Masoretic text. But it is also clearly not

Figure 68. Rekindling the Word: In search of Gospel truth by Carsten Peter Thiede (1995).

the Septuagint text. The translator made lots of different word choices. It's *a* translation of the Hebrew. But the Greek is very different from what we call the Septuagint. So just because people tell you the Dead Sea Scrolls have Greek, doesn't mean they're Septuagint Greek. That said, there *are* some fragments of texts that *do* match what we call the Septuagint.

Carsten Peter Thiede, author of *The Jesus Papyrus*, wrote in another of his books, *Rekindling the Word*, that there are six fragments with a few words that match what we call the Septuagint. Just six are called "reliably identified."

But he says, all the "Greek fragments can be dated to the period from the middle of the first century BC to the middle of the first century AD. This means that the Greek texts are the most recent of all manuscripts found in Qumran."[63]

So after all this investigation across centuries, all the scholars and all the investigation, and we end up with this? The oldest Greek words on a piece of papyrus or leather are only reliably dated to the 1st century, sometime before 68 AD, when the Roman conquerors came through Israel!

That does it. I cannot believe in a BC Septuagint. But I *can and do* believe there was **something** made in the 1st century AD. But let's remember what this means:

1. If there was no BC Septuagint, there was no acceptance of a BC Greek text. That means those Hebrew-speaking Hebrew synagogues in Israel used ... surprise! Hebrew!

2. If they used Hebrew in Israel —and even writers in Alexandria, including Origen, admitted this freely— then there is *no way* that Jesus or the apostles could have **quoted** the Septuagint. This means they did not quote or reference a Greek Apocrypha, either. Remember, only the Greek Septuagint included the Apocrypha as scripture, not the Hebrew, as even both Origen and Jerome admitted.

3. If there is *no way* that Jesus or the apostles could have quoted the Septuagint, then how come the Greek Septuagint has words and phrases similar to those used by Jesus and His apostles in the New Testament?

---

63) See *Rekindling the Word: in Search of Gospel Truth*, by Carsten Peter Thiede (Valley Forge, PA: Trinity Press International, 1995), pp. 160-161.

The Dead Sea Scrolls

Critics like to say that Jesus and the apostles were quoting the Septuagint Greek Old Testament. But actually, *it was the other way around*.

Whatever Greek Old Testament translations *were* made in the first century, were modified in the later 1st and early 2nd century, by people who had New Testament books *sitting right in front of them!* They wrote familiar New Testament words and phrases into their own copies of a Greek Old Testament. **POOF!** Jesus' and the apostles' words were now in a Greek text of the Old Testament – that was created in the later 1st or early 2nd century AD, probably for use by Alexandrian churches.[64]

So a Greek Old Testament *was* made during or after the life of Jesus.[65] Even if it came out, in Alexandria, by that late date, do you really think the Hebrews would abandon the Hebrew for an untested Greek that was so different from the Hebrew, as everyone admits? No way.

Let this sink in:

Jesus did not use the Septuagint. Neither did His apostles. They couldn't have.

So who DID create the Septuagint? And when? I can only go by the information that history has allowed us.

One guy had *motive*. He wanted to make the Hebrew Old Testament something he could play with, to make allegories and analogies, and to compare with Greek philosophy. For

---

64) Remember the Septuagint words in Psalm 13:3 (in English Bibles, Psalm 14:3), where Paul's words from Romans 1:13-18 are inserted into the text. And remember that Origen and Catholic scholars *admit it!*
65) It is easily possible that just the Genesis to Deuteronomy were translated during Jesus' lifetime. Then after that the other Old Testament books and Apocrypha were added.

that, he wanted and felt he needed a Greek Old Testament.

One guy had *means*. He was born wealthy. His family was contemporary with the Ptolemaic dynasty. He had both social and family connections to the Hasmonean and Herodian dynasties, and even the Julius-Claudius dynasty in Rome. He was educated in Roman, Greek and Egyptian culture, and in Judaism, especially.

And one guy had *opportunity*. He had access to the priests in Jerusalem, and could go back and forth as he pleased. He had visited the Temple in Jerusalem at least once. He was a representative of the Alexandrian Jewish community. And he seems to have had plenty of time to pull it off.

10

The Most Likely Suspect

The most likely suspect to have created the so-called Septuagint is none other than Philo of Alexandria, Thackeray's 6th witness, the one we set aside. He had **motive, means, and opportunity.** If Philo is the culprit, then he completed it **before** he passed away about 50 AD. He could have afforded to pay people to do the work for him.

The story would spread, because of his influence. Who would question him? Soon the fictional *"Letter" of Aristeas* (which Philo wrote?) would spread like wildfire all over the known world, to support the newly-made Greek Old Testament. The Alexandrians would particularly like it, since it eventually added in the Apocryphal "stories," all in one big book.

And there is ample time after that for Josephus (90s), then Aquila (120-130), Symmachus and Theodotion (both 170-200) to do their own work. And there is plenty of time for the Alexandrian religious people to mess with *that* Greek.

Then, well after the Alexandrian compromised "christians" accepted this as God's word, Origen came on the scene and started to check whether it matched the Hebrew. But he kept the results to himself and his peers. He passed on the lie that the Septuagint was "all from God" and that the Hebrew leaders had suppressed "the truth" of the Apocryphal writings. He couldn't admit what he clearly knew: that the Hebrew actually preserved God's words and the Greek was an obvious corruption of the Bible.

From this faulty foundation came the later Alexandrian Greek texts, the Alexandrinus, Vaticanus and Sinaiticus –regardless of when they were *actually* written. And this text by 405 AD became translated into the Roman Catholic Latin Vulgate, since the Catholic system of bondage so desperately needed the false doctrines contained in the Apocrypha.

And that set the stage for Satan's monstrous plot that was hatched in the 19th-20th centuries: to "fix" the preserved Bible and substitute a counterfeit Bible for all people, complete with Apocrypha. One world Bible for one world religion.

But we ***don't have to worry*** if there is **no BC Septuagint**. We have God's words, preserved from the Hebrew Old Testament and the Greek New Testament, then passed down and translated accurately, by the Levites and scribes and Jewish believers, to the Masoretes, in the Hebrew, and by the persecuted believers in Greek and other languages, all the way down to our King James Bible, God's preserved words in one book for us, in one language.

Now think about this. If this Greek Septuagint with Apocrypha ***isn't God's work***, then you can ***bet that the Devil*** is involved. What's the ***Devil's end game?*** I'll answer ***that*** in another book.

God bless you, and have a wonderful day.

Index

A

Africanus 38–40, 74, 84

Alexandria 10, 13, 30, 32–35, 37–38, 57, 60, 66, 68–73, 78, 85, 90, 94–96, 102–103, 105

Alexandrinus 18–19, 24, 29, 31–32, 40, 46, 86, 106

Ambrose 33

Anatolius of Laodicea 73

Antioch 77

Apocrypha 5–7, 9–10, 14, 17, 28, 30–31, 38–40, 44–46, 56, 75, 82–84, 96, 102–103, 106–107

Aquila 37, 84, 88, 106

Aristobulus 54–55, 70, 74

Augustine 29, 85–87, 91

B

Babylonian Talmud 53–54

Baruch 82, 87

Bel and the Dragon 87

Bible Societies 10, 45

Book of Mormon 15, 17, 28

Brigham Young 33

C

Caesarea Maritima 32, 56

Caesarion 65–66

Chrysostom 76–79, 81

Clement of Alexandria 34–35, 70–71

Cleopatra 65–66
Constantine, Emperor 7, 33, 56

D

De Principiis 13, 40
Dead Sea scrolls 41, 98, 101
Demetrius 55, 72, 94–96
Doctrine of Reserve 35–36
Douay-Rheims 10, 14, 16–17, 23–24, 27, 89–90

E

Ecclesiasticus (Sirach)
Epiphanius 79–82, 85, 91, 96
Epistle to the Laodiceans 88
Esdras 71, 88
Eusebius 33, 55–56, 73–76

F

Flavius Josephus 61–62
Frank Sadowski 13, 40
Fuller Seminary 31, 87

H

Hebrew Bible 10, 39, 75
Henry St. John Thackeray 47, 83, 93–94
Herod 65
Hexapla 14, 25, 29, 32, 35–37, 40, 46, 56, 84–87

I

Isis Unveiled 34

J

Jerome 27, 29, 80–81, 83, 85–91, 102

Joseph Smith 33
Julius Caesar 65
Justin Martyr 64, 66, 70

L

Lancelot Brenton 31, 46
Latin Vulgate 10, 14, 16–17, 27, 45, 80–81, 83, 85, 87, 89, 106
Leningrad Codex 41, 99
Leningradensis 41
Letter of Aristeas 11, 46–49, 53–55, 60, 63, 65, 68, 70, 74–75, 79, 83, 91–95, 98
Letter of Jeremiah 87
LXX 37, 79

M

Maccabees 87
Madame Blavatsky 34
Marc Antony 66
Masoretes 40–42, 106
Masoretic Text 10, 41, 101
Masseketh Sopherim 51–54
Megillath Taanith 49
Menedemus 73
Metobelus 37
Moses 34, 42, 51, 55–56, 58–60, 77, 91

N

Nahal Hever 99–101
New American Bible 28, 89–90

O

Obelus 37

Origen 12–15, 25–26, 29, 32–40, 42, 46, 56–57, 70, 73–74, 78, 80–81, 84–87, 102–103, 106

Oxford Movement 35

P

Palestinian Talmud 53

Pharos Island 59–60

Philadelphus 55, 58, 65–67, 69, 72, 74, 82, 94–97

Philo of Alexandria 57, 105

Plato 55–56

Platonists 34

Prayer of Manasses 88

Pseudo-Aristobulus 55, 74

Ptolemy 49–52, 55, 58, 65–67, 69–70, 72–76, 79, 91, 94–95

Purgatory 5–6, 10, 44

Q

Queen of Heaven 89

R

R. H. Charles 47

Rahlfs-Hanhart 24, 31

Roman Catholicism

S

Septuagint 6–7, 9–12, 14–18, 20, 24, 27–32, 36–37, 39, 44–49, 51, 53–56, 58, 61, 63–64, 66–71, 73–76, 78–81, 83–91, 94–96, 99–103, 105–107

Septuaginta 24–27, 31, 46, 101

Serapeum 73

Sinaiticus 9, 12, 14–15, 18–19, 21–23, 27, 29, 31–32, 40, 42, 44, 46, 86, 106

Sirach 82, 87
Song of the Three Young Men 87
Summer Institute of Linguistics 45
Susanna 39, 87
Symmachus 37, 84, 88, 106

T

Tertullian 55, 71–73, 75, 77, 80
Theodotion 37–38, 84, 86–88, 106
Tischendorf 12, 44
Titus 62

V

Vaticanus 9, 12, 15, 18–23, 27, 29, 31–32, 40, 46, 86, 106
Vespasian 62

W

Walter Walsh 35
Wisdom of Solomon 82, 87
Wycliffe Bible Translators 10

Made in United States
Troutdale, OR
08/22/2024